At Issue

Does Outsourcing Harm America?

Other Books in the At Issue Series:

At Issue

Does Outsourcing Harm America?

Lisa Krueger, Book Editor

GREENHAVEN PRESS
A part of Gale, Cengage Learning

GALE
CENGAGE Learning

Detroit • New York • San Francisco • New Haven, Conn • Waterville, Maine • London

Christine Nasso, *Publisher*
Elizabeth Des Chenes, *Managing Editor*

For more information, contact:
Greenhaven Press
27500 Drake Rd.
Farmington Hills, MI 48331-3535
Or you can visit our Internet site at gale.cengage.com

Articles in Greenhaven Press anthologies are often edited for length to meet page require-ments. In addition, original titles of these works are changed to clearly present the main thesis and to explicitly indicate the author's opinion. Every effort is made to ensure that Greenhaven Press accurately reflects the original intent of the authors. Every effort has been made to trace the owners of copyrighted material.

Cover image courtesy of Images.com/Corbis.

LIBRARY OF CONGRESS CATALOGING-IN-PUBLICATION DATA

Does outsourcing harm America? / Lisa Frohnapfel-Krueger, book editor.
      p. cm. -- (At issue)
    Includes bibliographical references and index.
    ISBN 978-0-7377-4673-0 (hbk.) -- ISBN 978-0-7377-4674-7 (pbk.)
    1. 1. Offshore outsourcing--Economic aspects--United States. 2. 2. United States--Commerce. 3. 3. United States--Economic conditions. I. I. Frohnapfel-Krueger, Lisa.
    HD2368.U6D64 2010
    330.973--dc22
                                                                                      2009038722

Printed in the United States of America
1 2 3 4 5 6 7 14 13 12 11 10

Contents

Introduction

In the 1980s, the U.S. manufacturing industry began to relocate jobs to other countries. The manufacturing industry saw such outsourcing as an opportunity to reduce payroll expenses because of the wage gap between industrialized and developing nations. As a result, layoffs in the U.S. manufacturing industry became commonplace. In the past several years, outsourcing has also penetrated the service and technology industries. Cheaper foreign labor is just one aspect of the outsourcing trend. Advances in technology, free trade, health insurance costs, environmental regulations, and a free flow of capital have also contributed to the growth of outsourcing. According to a 2004 article in the *Seattle Post-Intelligencer*, "It is unclear how many accounting, engineering, technical support and other professional jobs have moved offshore in recent years. But some industry watchers believe as many as 200,000 service jobs could be lost each year for the next 11 years."

In addition to the loss of U.S. jobs, outsourcing has also raised product-safety concerns. In 2007, millions of toys made in China were recalled because they contained lead paint. The recall brought attention to China's lax safety standards and the lack of regulations for imported goods. Consumers and some lawmakers are calling for tougher policies to reduce the numbers of unsafe products entering the United States. Outsourcing critics suggest U.S. companies are to blame by urging manufacturers and service providers to keep prices low. The critics believe the drive for the lowest price has resulted in corners being cut, resulting in unsafe products and shoddy service. Regardless of the cause, recalls and inadequate service have the potential to tarnish a company's brand image. As a result, some companies are revisiting their use of outsourcing.

While some companies have had bad outsourcing experiences, others have prospered. Outsourcing offers companies the opportunity to innovate and to create new processes. Supporters of outsourcing claim jobs lost in the United States can be replaced with more complex and better-paying positions. Through outsourcing, U.S. companies have the ability to focus on manufacturing products that generate high revenue, such as high-end computer chips and advanced software. Outsourcing to countries such as India have enabled U.S. companies to maximize revenues, reduce expenses, and obtain access to specialized skills and services; U.S. companies can focus on core business competencies and revenue-generating activities. In the meantime, U.S. companies that are not participating in outsourcing are staying competitive by having faster cycle times, focusing on customer service, and having reduced shipping costs.

Outsourcing is a phenomenon that creates a variety of economic, social, and legal concerns and was a hot topic during the 2008 presidential election. While on the campaign trail, Barack Obama stated, "We have to stop providing tax breaks for companies that are shipping jobs overseas and give those tax breaks to companies that are investing here in the United States of America." When fielding a question about the return of outsourced jobs, Obama stated, "Not all of these jobs are going to come back." The goal, he said, was to "go after the high-skill, high-wage jobs of the future" and create positions that cannot be outsourced to the lowest bidder. The outsourcing debate continues to be relevant. *At Issue: Does Outsourcing Harm America?* explores both the positive and negative aspects of outsourcing.

1

U.S. Corporations Can Benefit from Outsourcing

Melanie Rodier

Melanie Rodier is an associate editor for Wall Street & Technology *and a graduate of New York University and the University of Oxford.*

The economic downturn has prompted companies to look at outsourcing as a way to cut costs. In addition to cost benefits, outsourcing provides access to technology and expertise and the ability to focus on core products and services. Outsourcing also allows companies to add and remove people from projects as needed. However, companies should consider the costs of outsourcing before committing to a contract.

Amid the economic downturn, more and more Wall Street firms are considering outsourcing to cut costs as well as gain access to technology and expertise. But the shaky economy requires firms to do more outsourcing due diligence than ever before.

In today's tight economic environment, companies increasingly are turning to outsourcing as a way to cut costs. But experts suggest firms should carefully weigh the benefits, challenges and risks of sending work out to third parties before signing on the dotted line.

"We're seeing firms that wouldn't talk about outsourcing before talking about it now," relates Chris Connors, a director

Melanie Rodier, "Outsourcing in Volatile Times," *Wall Street & Technology*, vol. 27, January 2009, p. 30. Copyright ® 2009 United Business Media LLC. Reproduced by permission.

with investment management consulting firm Citisoft. "Everyone is looking at different ways to cut costs."

As budgets tighten across the financial industry, a key benefit of outsourcing is the ability to bring in a service provider on an ad hoc basis without adding to fixed operational costs, notes Glen Froio, president of Northpoint Solutions, which provides services such as management dashboards, investor reporting, analyst research, and portfolio and risk management analytics.

Service providers also offer firms access to capabilities, expertise and technology that they may not have in-house. Outsourcing providers often invest in the latest technology, offsetting the cost by sharing the technology among several clients.

As budgets tighten across the financial industry, a key benefit of outsourcing is the ability to bring in a service provider . . . without adding to fixed operational costs.

"When we started a mutual fund, it was very complex from an operational and regulatory standpoint," says Peter Mauthe, president of Dallas-based Rhoads Lucca Capital Management, which has multiple outsourcing partners, including Gemini Fund Services. "It made no sense to re-create internally what I could outsource externally. When I looked at the cost benefit, I could outsource to Gemini—to an organization that had experience, talent and technology that was as good or better than anything I could hope to create internally [and] that it made no sense to re-create."

Driving Growth

But outsourcing is more than a cost-saving strategy, adds Mauthe. More important, he says, outsourcing is a driver for growth. "It's a key factor in us being able to grow our business. It allows us to focus on what we do," Mauthe stresses. "We could increase the size of our company five-fold in revenue and only hire five or six more people, because we outsource so much of the really technological skills, such as accounting and IT [information technology]."

By outsourcing non-core functions, Rhoads Lucca can concentrate on its core business of investment management, rather than getting bogged down in operational services, adds Andrew Rogers, president of Gemini Fund Services, which works with advisers and funds to manage services such as fund accounting, compliance monitoring and reporting. "Advisers want to focus on managing and raising assets," Rogers says. "Most people don't create a fund to do back-office accounting but to raise assets. So where do you want to focus your energies? On the back office or on managing money? That's the biggest benefit of outsourcing."

Outsourcing allows a financial firm to transfer the risk of cost fluctuations to the vendor.

Rhoads Lucca has outsourced its entire IT infrastructure. According to the firm's Mauthe, the investment manager's infrastructure outsourcing partner, External IT, can provide greater reliability and expertise than Rhoads Lucca could build internally. The outsourcer also offers a help desk that is open 24 hours a day, seven days a week.

"Every once in a while something comes up—if you're in another part of the world, you don't have a help desk," Mauthe says. "So it's a key factor in us being able to grow our business. By outsourcing, our IT is available anywhere in the world."

Outsourcing the IT infrastructure also means having a solid business continuity plan, Mauthe adds. "If I came back to the office and my office building didn't exist anymore, it wouldn't stop us from operating for the rest of the day, as . . . all our IT infrastructure is outsourced and available on the Internet."

Citisoft's Connors suggests outsourcing also provides firms with increased flexibility. "This can be the flexibility to expand product offerings, if the service provider supports new products a client isn't already into," he says. "It also can help [firms] expand into new markets."

Perhaps most important in today's volatile markets, outsourcing allows a financial firm to transfer the risk of cost fluctuations to the vendor, says Stuart Levi, head of the information technology legal practice at Skadden, a New York–based law firm. "You can do this by having a fixed price for a number of units or paying X amount per employee," he explains. "You can work out a price and know you'll get that service for that price."

Another big benefit of outsourcing, according to Levi, is the ability to easily add and remove people from projects. "You can say to a vendor, 'I need this work done. I think I need 30 people,' and then a few months later you can change it to 27 people," he elaborates. "You can ramp up and down much more easily than with your own employees."

Look Before You Leap

Despite the obvious benefits of outsourcing, however, firms need to take a deep look at their costs before signing an outsourcing contract, experts say. "We encourage people to look at what their cost structure is," says Citisoft's Connors. "It's a myth that outsourcing is always cheaper. If you run your business in a lean way, it might not be the case."

He adds, "You really need to look at how much things are costing you versus how much it would cost to outsource. It's difficult to measure sometimes as you also have shared costs such as IT infrastructure or real estate that need to be factored in. You have to look across your operational environment and understand what things are really costing you now so that when the time comes to explore a vendor arrangement, it can really help save money."

Companies should also consider what they will look like to clients when services are outsourced, and ensure the roles and responsibilities of both the asset manager and the service provider are clear to everyone. "Make sure that what affects clients is kept in-house, such as reporting," notes Connors. If there are any differences in what clients will see with certain services, let them know that service has been outsourced, he adds.

One risk that companies must factor into the equation these days is the possibility that the outsourcing firm could face its own economic hardship. "There's a lot of concern now about doing business with a service provider who loses Lehman Brothers as a client, for example, and therefore loses ability to service you," relates Skadden's Levi.

Another challenge is ensuring that service levels meet expectations. Firms need to examine their service level agreements closely early on, Citisoft's Connors stresses. "Everything needs to be ironed out up front so there's no confusion on what is expected," he advises.

In the meantime, as companies tighten their belts, firms are increasingly looking at renegotiating their existing contracts, and COOs [chief operating officers] are scrutinizing contract lengths and pricing, says Skadden's Levi. "There's more interest in doing shorter-term deals and seeing how it goes," he contends.

"With a longer deal you're more locked into commitment," Levi says. "Our experience is that clients are a bit more reluctant to do longer-term agreements. No one is thinking too long-term in a lot of areas. People think they're not sure about their needs changing [in the future]. But they're concerned about volumes of business. And there are lots of things like that playing into it."

2

The Advantages of Outsourcing Are Eroding

John Ferreira and Len Prokopets

John Ferreira is executive director at Accenture, a global management consulting, technology services, and outsourcing company in New York City. Len Prokopets is a principal at Archstone Consulting, an organizational and strategic consulting firm for businesses in Stamford, Connecticut; he is author of "The Five Key Elements of World Class Supplier Relationship Management" and "Supplier Relationship Management—Maximizing the Value of Your Supply Base."

Manufacturers are finding the benefits of outsourcing to be not as pronounced as previously believed. The rising costs of transportation, the decline in value of the U.S. dollar, quality issues, logistics, and theft of intellectual property have contributed to manufacturers' reevaluating of the practice of outsourcing.

Just when thousands of manufacturers thought that offshoring a significant portion of their manufacturing and supply operations has given them competitive parity, the game may be changing again. The same factors that made offshoring a sure-fire tactic for reducing costs have shifted dramatically and now are eroding many of those savings. As a result, onshore and near-shore production is now viable and competitive in many cases.

You may want to hit the hold button before moving more of your supply operations off-shore; many manufacturers are finding that the numbers just don't add up anymore. In fact, a significant percentage of U.S. manufacturers are seriously reconsidering their production and sourcing strategies and even beginning to return manufacturing that they had once moved to low-cost countries.

The Way Things Were

Over the last 10 years, manufacturers have viewed offshoring as a necessity—one virtually mandated by the price demands of customers and by the cost advantages of competitors that had already aggressively off-shored. The rationale for offshoring was, in fact, a rather straightforward economic one. Suppliers in low-cost countries such as China have been able to offer "perceived" prices 25 to 40 percent lower than those available on shore—the typical threshold or tipping point for moving off shore. These reduced prices were made possible by low labor costs, cheap commodities, and favorable exchange rates.

Quality problems, longer supply chains, lack of visibility, piracy and intellectual capital theft are also part of the offshoring operation.

Many manufacturing executives now recognize, however, that quality problems, longer supply chains, lack of visibility, piracy and intellectual capital theft are also part of the offshoring operation, meaning that not all of the 25 to 40 percent off-shore sourcing savings goes to their bottom line. . . . In fact, the perceived offshoring cost advantage may have never really been that high and likely significantly less when "all-in" costs are considered.

In addition, offshoring has forced many manufacturers to pull back on competitive differentiation strategies based on customization of products and services to customer needs. Offshoring requires shipping container-size minimum orders and months-long order cycle times, thereby reducing the flexibility and responsiveness of companies' supply chains. With inflexible supply chains, companies are no longer able to effectively tailor products and services to unique customer and channel needs. Despite these issues, most executives believed that the sheer magnitude of the offshoring savings overcame the increased costs of doing business and loss of customer-centric capabilities.

However, recent changes in the economic environment have served to undermine the case for offshoring to low-cost countries. In some cases, in fact, the existing drawbacks of offshoring may now make this option the wrong decision in many cases.

Transportation charges for ocean freight are going through the roof, and many foreign currencies are gaining value compared to the U.S. dollar.

The Wake-Up Call

Off-shore labor and commodity costs are being hit by double-digit increases each year, transportation charges for ocean freight are going through the roof, and many foreign currencies are gaining in value compared to the U.S. dollar. Together, these factors are acting to make offshoring less attractive as a manufacturing and supply chain strategy for many manufacturers—especially when it comes to serving the large U.S. market.

Over the last three years alone (from 2005 through 2008), the costs of offshoring have increased across a broad range of indices:

• Ocean freight costs have increased 135 percent.

- The global commodity price index has risen by 27 percent.

- The Chinese yuan has gained 18 percent in value compared to the U.S. dollar.

- Chinese manufacturing wages have risen by 44 percent.

Recently, Archstone Consulting conducted an in-depth survey of thirty-nine senior executives from U.S. and European-based manufacturers to assess the evolving footprint of global manufacturing and supply networks.

According to that survey, 40 percent of manufacturing executives report experiencing a staggering increase of 25 percent or more in "core" direct costs on off-shored supply—materials, components, logistics and transportation—over the last three years. Almost 90 percent expect further significant ongoing price increases of 10 percent or more over the next 12 months of 10 percent or more (11 percent of manufacturers report that they expect core offshored costs to increase by over 20 percent).

The perceived advantages of offshoring may never have been as significant as thought.

While these trends will always have short-term fluctuations up and down, the longer-term trend line, according to many economists, points to two developments:

- The re-emergence of the U.S. and some near-shore manufacturing sources as attractive supply markets.

- The potential for the local U.S. supply base to regain some of the business lost to offshoring in recent years.

While it may be some time before the full implications of these trends is known, it's telling that many manufacturers already have come to realize that positioning manufacturing and supply closer to its customer markets can help overcome many of the "soft" issues associated with offshoring. This, combined with the eroding financial advantage of offshoring, is renewing manufacturers' interest in near-shore and on-shore supply and manufacturing.

Case in point: When a major specialty clothing retailer in the U.S. had difficulty matching its holiday inventories to demand due to the lengthy lead times required by its off-shore materials manufacturer, it shifted that manufacturing to an East Coast mill that was better able to meet demand with just-in-time efficiency. For the retailer, bringing manufacturing on-shore shortened its supply chain and improved supply chain visibility, enabling decisions to be made faster.

The True Off-Shore Cost

It appears, interestingly, that the perceived advantages of off-shoring may never have been as significant as thought. This is particularly so for manufacturers who sell their products to consumers at home in large domestic markets like the U.S. The actual cost advantage all along may never have been more than 15 percent—and for some products as little as 5 percent—when considering the "all-in" costs of offshoring as understood by applying a robust total cost model. After applying such a total cost model, manufacturers may find that much of the cost advantage of offshoring has been erased. For some products, in fact, off-shore supply might actually have a cost disadvantage!

An overwhelming majority—nearly 90 percent—of manufacturers are contemplating a change or have already changed their manufacturing and supply strategy.

Unfortunately, more than 60 percent of manufacturers that we surveyed apply only rudimentary total cost models, ignoring cost components that contribute up to 20 percent or more to the all-in cost of off-shored production. Many manufacturers look only at the most easily available cost components and therefore see a distorted picture of the relative costs of different manufacturing or sourcing options. . . .

A New Opportunity Emerges

The door is beginning to reopen for the migration of manufacturing to near- or on-shore. An overwhelming majority—nearly 90 percent—of manufacturers are contemplating a change or have already changed their manufacturing and supply strategy. When viewed in light of many manufacturers' all-too-recent drive to offshore operations as rapidly as possible, this is truly a striking change in direction.

Moderating a panel discussion on on-shoring at Northwestern University's Kellogg School of Management [in Evanston, Illinois, in 2008], Kevin Meyer, president and owner of Superfactory Ventures LLC [an online resource for manufacturing management] and president of Specialty Silicone Fabricators, a global manufacturer of silicone components for the medical device industry [both are in California], noted that 70 percent of attendees opted to attend the on-shoring seminar over a number of others on the program agenda.

"Imagine that," he reported on his blog, "that a contrarian subject like on-shoring being more popular than going green, sustainability, and especially merger and acquisition topics at a top-tier graduate management school; . . . it really comes down to the only true reason to off-shore is to get closer to the customer base."

As a *Business Week* article by Pete Engardio titled, "Can the U.S. Bring Jobs Back from China?" noted, "The economies of global trade are starting to tilt back in favor of the U.S. to a degree unseen in a generation."

A critical question many manufacturers will need to ask is: "Having off-shored our operations and supply networks, which ones should be returned on-shore or near-shore, and when?" Th[at] may be difficult to answer, and will be different for every manufacturer and product. Thirty percent of executives report contemplating some change, while 59 percent are changing their strategy. Of those changing strategies, 26 percent are relocating manufacturing and sourcing and 33 percent are being more selective in making offshoring decisions.

One of the key impacts of the offshoring challenges is the need to rebalance manufacturing and supply networks. This re-balancing includes a shift of manufacturing to North America from China and other regions. Companies' manufacturing and supply plans for the next three years (according to the Archstone/SCMR survey) indicate that North American manufacturing stands to grow 5 percent over and above local market demand. This expected increase is the largest in the world and represents a market reversal of offshoring. These plans also indicate that China manufacturing will decline by 2 percent relative to local market demand as North American offshoring declines and as lower-cost production moves to Eastern Europe, India and other Asian countries.

With more manufacturing and supply networks migrated back to the U.S. or near-shore, emphasis can again be placed on market and product strategies—product development, new channel integration, and meeting customer expectations for value, service, timeliness and innovation, not just low cost.

Comments from three executives who were surveyed on their future manufacturing and supply plans highlight these trends:

- "There is serious consideration being given here for near-shore (Canada/Mexico) and on-shore operations in lower-wage states like Arkansas and Alabama, etc."

- "Our supply chain management group is developing new sources in North America to replace that lost during the last wave of offshoring."

- "We are considering the fact that our customers require on-time delivery and the fact that we can charge a premium for that if we can deliver consistently on short-fuse needs."

Barriers to Moving Forward

It is prudent to note some barriers to re-establishing sourced or production capabilities on-shore or near-shore. The migration over the years of manufacturing off-shore has decimated the local manufacturing infrastructure and its highly skilled engineering and technical workforce, including many skilled shop-floor maintenance workers. Much of the supplier networks that served those industries have disappeared as well.

Re-establishing a manufacturing footprint in the U.S. will require a strong commitment and investment.

Re-establishing a manufacturing footprint in the U.S. will require a strong commitment and investment to rebuild the critical capabilities. Workforce availability and skills, site planning, construction, and infrastructure rebuilding to support operations won't be easy or accomplished quickly. Capital to rebuild may be difficult to access and federal, state and local tax incentives and other support will be required. Additionally, manufacturers will need to identify and develop a network of nearby suppliers with the appropriate capabilities and capacity.

Manufacturers looking at moving operations and supply networks back home should also carefully assess their internal operational capabilities—are those capabilities intact, or have they been outsourced and supporting assets and skill sets lost? Can the capabilities be re-established here, by whom, and how soon? Manufacturers also report that a new internal "mindset" is necessary to fully capitalize on the new economic dynamics of bringing production and supply on- or near-shore—specifically companies cited the following as important:

- Becoming very effective at developing a network of capable local suppliers.

- Building the internal capability to correctly analyze the total, all-in cost of their manufacturing and supply options.

- Developing a comprehensive manufacturing and supply strategy to guide individual sourcing and supply decisions.

A Framework for Success

As we have indicated, the evolving global footprint of manufacturing and supply networks may be changing again, in favor of the U.S. As part of your planning, we suggest approaching your manufacturing and supply sourcing decisions from a holistic perspective: evaluating the company's market and customer demands and competitive strategy against a clear and comprehensive understanding of total cost.

Manufacturing or sourcing at home or closer to home may create a competitive cost advantage, but it may also allow something more important—enabling your company to differentiate itself by tailoring products, offerings, and services to the multiple customer segments and channels you serve. Enabling this type of improved customer responsiveness is likely to increase revenue while decreasing cost—a powerful competitive advantage.

3

Outsourcing Has Contributed to the Loss of Manufacturing Jobs

Susan Helper

Susan Helper is the AT&T professor of economics at Case Western Reserve University in Cleveland, Ohio.

The United States has lost manufacturing jobs at an alarming rate to low-wage countries. However, many manufacturers are finding the advantages of outsourcing eaten up by hidden costs. The rising cost of transportation, supply-chain delays, and communication barriers are just some of the issues experienced by manufacturers that outsource. Many U.S. companies are finding they can compete with low-wage countries by developing strategies that draw on the knowledge and skills of all workers.

The United States has been losing manufacturing jobs at a stunning rate: 16% of the jobs disappeared in just the three years between 2000 and 2003, with a further decline of almost 4% since 2003 [through 2008]. In all, the nation has lost 4 million manufacturing jobs in just more than 8 years. This was some of the best-paying work in the country: The average manufacturing worker earns a weekly wage of $725, about 20% higher than the national average. Although manufacturing still pays more than average, wages have fallen relative to the rest of the economy, especially for non-college[-educated] workers. Manufacturing also employs significant

Susan Helper, "The High Road for U.S. Manufacturing," *Issues in Science & Technology*, vol. 25, Winter 2009, pp. 39–45. Copyright © 2009. University of Texas at Dallas. All rights reserved. Reproduced by permission.

numbers of white-collar workers: One in five manufacturing employees is an engineer or manager.

Continued hemorrhaging is not inevitable. The United States could build a high-productivity, high-wage manufacturing sector that also contributes to meeting national goals such as combating climate change and rebuilding sagging infrastructure. The country can do this by adopting a "high-road" production system that harnesses everyone's knowledge—from production workers to top executives—to produce high-quality innovative products.

Promoting High-Road Strategies

Promoting high-road strategies will strengthen manufacturing and the U.S. economy as a whole. Through coordination with highly skilled workers and suppliers, firms achieve high rates of innovation, quality, and fast response to unexpected situations. The resulting high productivity allows firms to pay fair wages to workers and fair prices to suppliers while still making fair profits.

How can this be done? Start with more investment in education, training, and R&D [research and development]. But education alone will not allow firms to overcome the market failures that block the adoption of efficient high-road practices. Nor will it reinvigorate income growth, which even for college-educated men has risen only 0.5% annually since 1973 at the median. Similarly, increased R&D spending by itself won't get innovative products to market.

More is needed. Competing with low-wage nations is not as daunting as one might think. Research by the Michigan Manufacturing Technology Center [a nonprofit organization that offers training and consulting services to small and mid-sized manufacturers in Michigan] suggests that most manufacturers have costs within 20% of their Chinese competitors. Reducing costs by this magnitude is well within the range achievable by high-road programs, and a key institution that can help bridge this gap is already in operation. The federal Manufacturing Extension Partnership (MEP) program teaches companies to develop new products, find new markets, and operate more efficiently—and it pays for itself in increased tax revenue from the firms it helps. This program will not save all the manufacturing at risk, but it will increase the viability of much of it, while increasing the productivity and wages of those who perform this important work.

Two main forces have caused U.S. manufacturing employment to fall: the growth of productivity during a period of stagnant demand and the offshoring of work to other nations, especially China. Economists differ as to the relative contribution of the two forces, but as Nobel Laureate Paul Krugman argued in the *Brookings Papers on Economic Activity* [a biannual journal by the public-policy think-tank the Brookings Institution], there is growing consensus that both are important. . . .

U.S. firms can and do compete with China and other low-wage countries, in part because direct labor costs are only 5 to 15% of total costs in most manufacturing. Many U.S. firms have costs not so different from those of Chinese firms. Therefore, it is not naïve to think that manufacturing can and should play an important role in the U.S. economy during the next several decades.

U.S. companies can continue to pay higher wages for direct labor and offset the added cost with greater capabilities.

A 2006 study by the Performance Benchmarking Service (PBS) suggests that most small U.S. manufacturers are competitive with Chinese firms or could become so. Similarly, a 2004 McKinsey study[by the McKinsey Global Institute, an economics research group] found that in many segments of the automotive parts industry, the "China price" is only 20 to

30% lower than the U.S. price for a similar component. Note that neither this study nor the PBS study takes into account most of the hidden costs discussed below. Thus, low-wage countries are not necessarily low-cost countries. U.S. companies can continue to pay higher wages for direct labor and offset the added cost with greater capabilities—capabilities that lead to outcomes such as higher productivity, fewer quality problems, and fewer logistical problems.

Offshoring Has Hidden Costs

Unfortunately, firms are handicapped in deciding where they should locate production because they often do not take into account the hidden costs of offshoring. A number of studies have found that most firms, even large multinationals, use standard accounting spreadsheets to make sourcing decisions. These techniques focus on accounting for direct labor costs, even though these are a small percentage of total cost, and ignore many other important costs.

Consider some of the hidden costs of having suppliers far away. First, top management is distracted. Setting up a supply chain in China and learning to communicate with suppliers requires many long trips and much time, time that could have been spent on introducing new products or processes at home. Second, there is increased risk from a long supply chain, especially with just-in-time inventory policies. Third, there are increased coordination and "handoff costs" between U.S. and foreign operations. More difficult communication among product design, engineering, and production hinders serendipitous discovery of new products and processes. Quality problems may be harder to solve because of geographic and cultural distance. Time to market may increase.

These costs can be substantial: One study by FANUC, a [Japanese] robotics manufacturer, found that they added 24% to the estimated costs of offshoring. The challenges of dealing with a far-flung supply base make it difficult for firms to innovate in ways that require linked design and production processes. For example, one Ohio firm had based its competitive advantage on its ability to quickly add features to its products (cup holders in riding mowers, to take a nonautomotive example). But when they sourced to China, these last-minute changes wreaked havoc with suppliers, and the firm was forced to freeze its designs much earlier in the product development process.

Why would firms systematically ignore these costs? One reason is to convince outside investors that the company is serious about reducing costs by taking actions that are publicly observable, such as shutting factories in the United States and moving to countries with demonstrably lower wages. However, as the U.S.-China price differential shrinks because of exchange rate revaluations, higher Chinese wages, and increased transportation costs, firms (such as Caterpillar) are turning more to suppliers closer to home.

Many U.S. firms can close the remaining cost gap with low-wage competitors. Some firms are already doing so, and there is evidence that a few widely applicable and teachable policies account for much of their success. . . .

U.S. firms cannot compete by imitating China by cutting wages and benefits. Instead, they should build on their strength by drawing on the knowledge and skills of all workers.

U.S. firms cannot compete by imitating China by cutting wages and benefits. Instead, they should build on their strengths by drawing on the knowledge and skills of all workers. Many of this country's high-productivity firms prospered by adopting a high-road production recipe in which firms, their employees, and suppliers work together to generate high productivity. Successful adoption of these policies requires that everyone in the value chain be willing and able to share knowledge. Involving workers and suppliers and using information technology (IT) are key ways of doing this.

Workers, particularly low-level workers, have much to contribute because they are close to the process: They interact with a machine all day, or they observe directly what frustrates consumers. For example, a study of steel-finishing lines by Casey Ichniowski, Kathryn Shaw, and Giovanna Prennushi found that firms with high-road practices had 6.7% more uptime (generating $2 million annually in net profits for a small plant) than did lines without them. The increase in uptime is due to communication and knowledge overlap. In a firm that does not use high-road practices, all communication may go through one person. In contrast, in high-road facilities, such as the one run by members of the United Steelworkers at Mittal Steel in Cleveland, workers solve problems more quickly because they communicate with each other directly in a structured way.

Involving suppliers is also important. Take, for example, the small supplier to Honda that had problems with some plastic parts. On an irregular basis, parts would emerge from molding machines with white spots along the edge of the product or molds not completely filled in. These problems, which had long plagued the company, were not solved until Honda organized problem-solving groups that pooled the diverse capacities and experiences of people in the supplier's plant. They quickly solved the problem. Molding machine operators noticed condensation dripping into the resin container from an exhaust fan in the ceiling, quality control technicians then saw that the condensation was creating cold particles in the resin, and skilled trade people designed a solution. . . .

A key reason why the high road's linked information flow is so powerful is that real production rarely takes place exactly according to plan. A manufacturing worker may be stereotyped as someone who pushes the same button every 20 seconds, day after day, year after year, but even in mature industries, this situation rarely occurs. For example, temperatures change, sending machines out of adjustment; customers change their orders; a supplier delivers defective parts; a new product is introduced. All of these contingencies mean that the perfect separation of brain work and hand work envisioned by efficiency guru Frederick Taylor [1856–1915] does not occur. . . .

Creating Discussion Forums

High-road production techniques have been codified and shown to work. But this process of codification takes a long time. How will the next generation of programs be developed? In addition, the exact ingredients of the high-road recipe vary by industry and over time. Thus, it is useful to have forums for discussion so that industry participants can make coordinated investments, both subsidized and on their own. The forums could elicit the detailed information necessary to design good policies, thus avoiding government failure. However, organizing the forums is subject to market failures, because the benefits of coordinated investment are diffuse and thus hard for a profit-making entity to capture.

Federal and state governments could establish competitive grant programs in which industries compete for funding to establish such forums. Also, MEP should encourage cities and regions to apply to create such forums. A large literature, including case studies and statistical work, has found that firms concentrated in the same geographical area (including customers, suppliers, rivals, and even firms in unrelated industries) are more productive. The advantages of geographical proximity include the ability to pool trained workers and the ease of sharing new ideas. These advantages can be magnified if institutions are created that organize these exchanges, facilitating the communication and development of trust.

Several prototypes of these discussion forums already exist in a number of stages of the value chain, including innovation

(Sematech), upstream supply [the Program for Automotive Renaissance in Tooling (PART) in Michigan], component supply (Accelerate in Wisconsin), and integrated skills training (the Wisconsin Regional Training Partnership and the Manufacturing Skills Standards Council). . . .

A bill to encourage the formation of discussion forums was introduced by U.S. Senators Sherrod Brown (D-OH) and Olympia Snowe (R-ME) in the summer of 2008. Called the Strengthening Employment Clusters to Organize Regional Success (SECTORS) Act, the legislation would provide grants of up to $2.5 million each for "partnerships that lead to collaborative planning, resource alignment, and training efforts across multiple firms" within an industry cluster.

It is much cheaper to act now to preserve the manufacturing capacity we have than to try to reconstruct it once it's gone.

Expanding MEP and creating discussion forums would cost about $300 million. I have calculated that if just half the firms increase their productivity by 20% as a result (the low estimate from [U.S. Census Bureau economic researcher] Ronald Jarmin's study of MEPs effectiveness) and can therefore compete with China, the United States would save 50,000 jobs at a cost of only $6,000 per job, a cost that would be offset by increased tax revenue. This $300 million is a tiny amount of money. State and local governments currently spend $20 to $30 billion on tax abatements to lure firms to their jurisdictions. That spending generally does not improve productivity. Moreover, it is much cheaper to act now to preserve the manufacturing capacity we have than to try to reconstruct it once it's gone.

This $300 million expenditure can also be compared with that for agricultural extension: $430 million in 2006 for an industry that employs 1.9% of the workforce and produces

0.7% of gross domestic product (GDP). In contrast, manufacturing is 10% of the workforce and 14% of GDP.

Paving the High Road

A number of observers have noted the fragility of high-road production in the United States. Cooperation, especially between labor and management, may flourish for a while but then collapse, or cooperation may be limited because management wants to keep its options open regarding the future of the facility. Low-road options (either in the United States or in low-wage nations overseas) remain attractive to firms, even if they impose costs on society. After a few failures, unions often become reluctant to trust again. Similar problems plague customer/supplier relations.

Therefore, we must look at broader economic policies that affect the stability of the high road in manufacturing and in other sectors. These policies can be divided into those that "pave the high road" (reduce costs for firms that choose this path) and those that "block the low road" (increase costs for firms that choose the low road, thus reducing their ability to undercut more socially responsible competitors).

With the right policies, the United States can have a revitalized manufacturing sector that brings with it good jobs, rapid innovation, and the capacity to pursue national goals.

Some examples of policies that pave the high road are universal health care, increased funding of innovation, and investments in training. Some policies that block the low road would be including in trade agreements protections for workers and the environment and strengthened safety regulations for workplaces and consumer products. Implementing these policies would require large investments but would benefit the entire economy, not just manufacturing.

Coordinated public effort to develop productive capabilities in the United States is an effective way of confronting the twin problems of shrinking manufacturing and stagnant income for most U.S. workers. With the right policies, the United States can have a revitalized manufacturing sector that brings with it good jobs, rapid innovation, and the capacity to pursue national goals.

Rather than abandon manufacturing, the nation can transform it into an example for the rest of the economy. The rationale for high-road policies is applicable to most industries in the United States. The policies outlined here could ensure that all parts of the economy remain strong and that all Americans participate in a productive way and reap the rewards of their efforts.

Many U.S. firms can close the remaining cost gap with low-wage competitors. Some firms are already doing so, and there is evidence that a few widely applicable and teachable policies account for a lot of their success.

Several in-depth studies have found that MEP pays for itself in increased tax revenue generated by the firms it serves. MEP could be even more effective if its scope were expanded, so that it could link together the disparate skills that firms must learn to master high-road production.

Outsourcing Harms the U.S. Middle Class

Dennis Behreandt

Dennis Behreandt has served as a managing editor of and is a long-time contributor to the New American *magazine, a publication of the John Birch Society, a libertarian political advocacy organization. Behreandt holds an undergraduate degree in history with a minor in biology and has studied Catholic theology at the graduate level.*

The 1950s were a time of growth and prosperity in the United States, and many people were living the American dream due to the abundance of manufacturing jobs. Today, policies favoring outsourcing mean manufacturing jobs in the United States have become scarce. The loss of manufacturing jobs has resulted in fewer Americans realizing the American dream.

All anyone needs to know about the 1950s in America can be inferred from the automobiles produced in 1959. Even the most pedestrian of commuter appliances turned out by Detroit that year were vehicular sculptures—equivalent, in some sense, to the soaring spires of Europe's Gothic cathedrals. Where those cathedrals in their vaulted naves sought to uplift the eyes and the spirit toward the promise of Heaven, American automakers in 1959 sought to embody in the automobile the confident optimism of the preceding decade.

Dennis Behreandt, "Losing Our Way: Once the Heart and Soul of America, the Middle Class Has Recently Endured Mounting Job Losses and Declining Standards of Living," *The New American*, vol. 23, June 25, 2007, pp. 8–12. Copyright © 2007 American Opinion Publishing Incorporated. Reproduced by permission.

On even the least pretentious of the era's cars, oceans of chrome swept back along highly sculpted body panels rising toward the rear in ostentatious tail-fins. From the rear, oversized taillights blazed forth a bright red glow in shapes and forms intended to invoke the forward-thinking technical achievements of the jet age or the power and glory of the rocketry that was about to put men into space.

The U.S. Manufacturing Industry

In 1959, the automobile, whether a Ford, Chevy, or Chrysler, was the quintessential American symbol of optimism, hope, and greatness—an exuberant message in steel and glass proclaiming to the world that America was at the pinnacle of its strength and greatness.

There was good cause for the optimism. In his 1986 history of the decade, entitled *God's Country: America in the Fifties*, historian J. Ronald Oakley pointed out that during the years of the fifties, "the United States enjoyed a period of unprecedented prosperity, consumerism, and economic optimism." It was a time when there seemed to be a job for anyone who wanted to work, when revolutionary labor-saving devices became available and affordable to nearly everyone, and when the world depended on U.S. economic might. According to Oakley, "At the middle of the decade the United States, with 6 percent of the world's population and 7 percent of the area produced almost half of the world's manufactured products," a trend driving a widespread prosperity with real wages for workers rising by 30 percent over the course of the decade. That powerhouse economy made it possible for even someone with a modest high-school education to enter the workforce and earn enough to buy a home, put a new car or two in the driveway, and raise a family, with the wife able to stay home and be a full-time mom. In the 1950s, *Leave It to Beaver* [a television show featuring a stereotypical 1950s family] was a reality. "Never, it seemed, had so many had it so good, and never had so many expected it to get better," Oakley concluded. "To many observers of the American scene, the old adage, 'The poor will always be with us,' was a thing of the past."

For the first time in American history, except perhaps the Great Depression, families today are worse off than their parents.

How times change. Now, almost 50 years after Detroit celebrated the American achievement via the medium of automotive coachwork, the workers of America's broad middle class face an uncertain future. For the first time in American history, except perhaps the Great Depression, families today are worse off than their parents. According to a recent report by the Economic Mobility Project created by the Pew Charitable Trusts, "Men in their 30s today earn less than men in their fathers' generation, and family income growth has slowed." The plight of the middle class is everywhere evident inside the nation's "big box" retail stores. Shelves are stocked with items bearing stickers proclaiming "made in China" while one looks almost in vain for anything labeled "made in America." Cheap foreign labor—sometimes even slave labor—produces the goods once made by Americans, and the middle class in this country has paid the price in unprecedented job losses that might never be recovered.

Offshoring America

Jaithirth Rao is an entrepreneur in the great American fashion with one exception: he conducts business in Bangalore, India. Until 2006, Rao, an accountant by trade, ran the Indian accounting firm MphasiS that makes its money by, among other things, processing portions of tax returns sent them by American accounting firms. He is currently the chairman of the company's board of directors. Rao's story is told by author

Thomas Friedman in his book *The World Is Flat,* which documents the rise of outsourcing and offshoring in the global economy. Interviewing Rao, Friedman asked, hypothetically: "I got my CPA. I work in a big accounting firm. . . . What is going to happen to me in this system" of outsourcing and offshoring American jobs?

The Indian businessman's reply was revealing. "We must be honest about it," said Rao who received his master's degree from the University of Chicago. "In ten years we are going to be doing a lot of the stuff that is being done in America today." This answer points to a disturbing trend.

At the beginning of the outsourcing and offshoring movement, now 20 years ago or more, the first jobs impacted were in high-paying manufacturing industries like automobiles and electronics. When those jobs disappeared, Americans looking for work switched to white-collar service-sector jobs, some of which—in accounting and in some healthcare fields—paid nearly as much or even more than the old manufacturing jobs that were lost. The greatest growth, though, came in lower-level service jobs, like call centers, that absorbed an influx of workers displaced from America's shuttered manufacturers. But now, as Rao pointed out, all those jobs—from accounting to customer service and others—are the next to be offshored.

That includes jobs in healthcare that many American middle-class workers have come to count on. After interviewing Rao, Friedman writes, he received an e-mail from William Brody, the president of Johns Hopkins University. In his e-mail, republished in Friedman's book, Brody describes an offshoring trend in the field of radiology. "I have just learned that in many small and some medium-sized hospitals in the US, radiologists are outsourcing reading of CAT scans to doctors in India and Australia!!!" Brody wrote. "Most of this evidently occurs at night (and maybe weekends) when the radiologists do not have sufficient staffing."

While that sounds like a good way to make sure that both doctors and patients are served with vital radiological information in a timely fashion, it really points to the fact that hospitals are choosing to outsource and offshore work that could be done by American workers. The lesson is that no one is safe. "Any activity where we can digitize and decompose the value chain, and move the work around will get moved around," Rao warns. "Some people will say, 'Yes, but you can't serve me a steak.' True, but I can take the reservation for your table sitting anywhere in the world. . . . In other words, there are parts of the whole dining-out experience that we can decompose and outsource."

The impact of job loss is far-reaching: individuals, families and the entire community have all been negatively touched.

The losses caused by such pervasive outsourcing and offshoring efforts are not just statistics—real people are hurt and real American communities are damaged. That was the lesson taught, according to professor Leslie Hossfeld of the University of North Carolina at Wilmington, by the closure of the Converse shoe factory in Robeson County, North Carolina, in 2001. That factory was the last Converse facility in America when the company, hammered by losses in the wake of NAFTA [the North American Free Trade Agreement], went bankrupt. The closure was the last straw, so to speak, in a county that, like many others in the United States, had seen manufacturers leave in droves since 1993 in order to start operations overseas.

According to Hossfeld, those losses have had a ripple effect throughout the region. "The impact of job loss is far-reaching: individuals, families and the entire community have all been negatively touched. Distress extends not only from the loss of jobs, but also from the more profound loss of an entire way of life." The pain is evident in the stories from the area.

"I've begged, I've totally begged, you know, for help to get me straightened out so I could go back to work," one displaced worker told Hossfeld, "but everywhere I went I've just been turned away. We can't help you. And I said, you know, it's a shame, I've worked all my life. Now I need some help and I can't get it." A person described as a "Robeson County agency worker" told Hossfeld: "We have family members, people, employees of the organization whose families have worked in the textile industries that have lost their jobs. . . . Every time somebody loses their job, they're losing health insurance for their family. If they have to choose between going to the doctor or putting food on the table they're going to put food on the table versus going to the doctor. Families need steady work."

The Endangered Middle Class

Robeson County is on the front lines of what has, according to CNN anchor Lou Dobbs, become a war on the middle class. According to Dobbs, that war is being carried out by elected officials [pre-2006] who as a group, for perhaps the first time in history, are no longer interested in putting the good of America and the welfare of American citizens first. "We are witnessing something that would have been unimaginable a quarter century ago: the emergence of a House of Representatives and a Senate that ignore the will of the majority of Americans, the middle class," Dobbs writes in his most recent book, *War on the Middle Class.* Instead, these representatives and the special interests they pander to, are increasingly "committed to a world order that views national sovereignty and borders as inconvenient impediments to trade and commerce, and our citizens as nothing more than consumers or units of labor in a global marketplace."

Considered as no more than "consumers," citizens are shorn of their humanity and become little more than statistics to be manipulated. That manipulation has resulted in incredible economic damage this decade with lives irrevocably altered and families pressured like never before by job loss. As Dobbs points out, "the twenty-first century began ... with more than three million manufacturing jobs lost in the first five years of this new century."

The twenty-first century began ... with more than three million manufacturing jobs lost in the first five years of this new century.

As Jaithirth Rao explained to Thomas Friedman, American workers and the middle-class families they support are by no means out of the woods. Unless something is done to reverse the policies that are destroying the livelihoods of millions of Americans, the economic future will become increasingly uncertain. "Unfortunately, a rapidly changing post-modern economy is less uplifting, and is putting more downward pressure on millions of our fellow Americans," Dobbs laments. "For the first time in our history, Americans aren't dreaming of a better life for their children—they are desperately hoping that their children won't be forced into a lower standard of living and lower quality of life."

Today, almost 50 years after Detroit's assembly lines produced the optimistic rolling sculptures that marked the heyday of the American automobile, historians look back and marvel at the achievements of America during the fifties. Tomorrow, 50 years in the future, historians might just look back on the world of today and marvel at the wrongheaded and dangerous policies that wiped out the last vestiges of America's heart and soul—the middle class.

5

Americans Are Offered Services at a Lower Cost Through Outsourcing

Douglas A. Irwin

Douglas A. Irwin holds a PhD in economics from Columbia University in New York City. Irwin has authored The Battle over Protection: A History of U.S. Trade Policy; Free Trade Under Fire; Against the Tide: An Intellectual History of Free Trade, *and* Managed Trade: The Case Against Import Targets.

Outsourcing service-sector jobs will allow companies to become more specialized while at the same time improving their efficiency and productivity. As a result, U.S. consumers will be offered services at a lower cost and companies will benefit from the extra income generated abroad. Policies regulating service-sector trade would hinder the ability of U.S. companies to compete in the global marketplace.

"The United States will be a Third World country in 20 years." So intoned Paul Craig Roberts, a former Reagan administration Treasury official and supply-side economist, at a Brookings Institution briefing earlier this month [January 2004]. Mr. Roberts makes this prediction because of white-collar job losses due to the outsourcing of service sector employment to India and China. As a result, whole classes of high-wage service sector employees—from software programmers to radiologists—now find themselves in competition with highly skilled workers abroad who earn a fraction of their U.S. counterparts.

Mr. Roberts also teamed up with Sen. Charles Schumer, a Democrat, to suggest in the *New York Times* that "the case for free trade is undermined by changes in the global economy." The fears they expressed about the service sector were eerily reminiscent of the early '90s, when Ross Perot insisted that NAFTA [the North American Free Trade Agreement] would hollow out America and produce a "great sucking sound" of jobs being siphoned off to low-wage Mexico. The conservative Mr. Roberts and the liberal Sen. Schumer are the most politically incongruous team of trade analysts since Patrick Buchanan and Ralph Nader opposed NAFTA a decade ago. Fortunately, just like their predecessors, their analysis is wrong.

The service sector, which traditionally has been insulated from international competition, is now ripe for outsourcing on a global scale.

Outsourcing Will Transform the Service Sector

The unlikely bedfellows are right in that the world is changing. The service sector, which traditionally has been insulated from international competition, is now ripe for outsourcing on a global scale. According to McKinsey [the McKinsey Global Institute, an economics research group], about 90% of the value of services output is now produced within the providing firm, but they expect this share to drop to 60% in 10 years. High-tech firms such as IBM are now outsourcing software programming to India, and medical centers are relying on Indian doctors to process data, to say nothing of the loss of America's call centers.

What will the service sector look like as a result of these developments? Some clues come from manufacturing, which already has been vastly reshaped. Outsourcing has transformed manufacturing from vertically integrated production structures to highly fragmented ones. Fifty years ago, Detroit's River Rouge plant sucked in iron and coal at one end and spat out an automobile at the other. Now, auto firms source component parts from a vast array of domestic and foreign suppliers.

Has U.S. manufacturing been vaporized in the process? No—manufacturing production has risen about 40% over the past decade. Despite lower wages abroad, foreign firms have chosen to produce cars made by high-wage workers here, including Honda in Ohio, Mercedes-Benz in Alabama, BMW in South Carolina and Toyota in California. Of course, the share of the American workforce in manufacturing has fallen steadily over the [post–World War II] period due to vast increases in productivity, but this is a world-wide phenomenon. Between 1995 and 2002, China, Japan, Brazil and other countries lost more manufacturing jobs than did the U.S., according to an Alliance Capital Management [a global investment management firm] study.

The Benefits of Service Sector Outsourcing

The service sector will be reshaped by international developments, too. But just as low-wage China has not taken all of our manufacturing capability, low-wage India is not going to take all of our service sector production. Service producers will become even more specialized and will have to seek new ways of improving their efficiency and productivity. (Productivity in the service sector has notoriously lagged behind that in manufacturing.) As long as the American workforce retains its high level of skills, and remains flexible as firms position themselves to improve their productivity, the high-value portion of the service sector will not evaporate.

Besides, while Messrs. Roberts and Schumer and others focus on the issue of displaced workers, they have completely ignored the efficiency benefits of service sector outsourcing.

As many businesses themselves purchase services, their lower costs will result in savings that can be passed on to consumers.

First, consumers will be provided with the services they demand, at lower prices. As many businesses themselves purchase services, their lower costs will result in savings that can be passed on to consumers. If a capable radiologist in India can read x-ray pictures at a quarter of the cost of doing so domestically, important health-care services can be delivered at lower cost to everyone, putting a brake on exploding medical costs.

Second, U.S. exporters of goods and services will benefit from the extra income generated abroad. The outsourcing of services to India counts in the U.S. balance of payments as an import of services. If we are going to start importing large amounts of such services, these imports must be paid for by exports of something. The dollars being spent by firms to purchase these services will come back to the U.S. either in the form of demand for U.S. goods (our exports to India) or foreign investment in the U.S. As McKinsey has noted, "[service] providers in low-wage countries require U.S. computers, telecommunications equipment, other hardware and software. In addition, they also procure legal, financial, and marketing services from the U.S."

Indeed, the U.S. is a major exporter of services, accounting for nearly a fifth of the world's trade in services. Services amount to nearly 30% of the value of all U.S. exports. Last year [2003], when the U.S. had about a $550 billion deficit in goods trade, we racked up nearly a $60 billion surplus in trade in services.

The Significance of Free Trade

Of course, importing services can create difficulties for some firms and their workers who are undergoing the process of adjusting to a new way of doing business. Specialization becomes much more refined across different economic activities, and can change quickly with shifts in technology. Messrs. Roberts and Schumer claim that comparative advantage and the old rules of trade no longer apply in today's world of mobile factors of production. But it is technology—not the movement of labor—that is creating new opportunities for trade in services, and this does not undermine the case for free trade and open markets.

To their credit, Messrs. Roberts and Schumer do not advocate what they call "old fashioned protectionism." Indeed, it appears that policymakers have few direct options to halt this process of technological change. Unfortunately, however, several state governments are considering laws that limit contracting with businesses that outsource from developing countries. Labor unions, such as the Communications Workers of America, have been lobbying Congress to follow suit.

Yet penalizing firms that import foreign-produced services is not an attractive option. If such imports help high technology and other service firms become more efficient, then forbidding U.S. companies from doing that when their foreign rivals are free to do it will only handicap U.S. firms. As American firms themselves are facing difficult competitive challenges from foreign producers, this would be like forcing them to fight with one hand tied behind their back.

Rather than penalizing firms, outsourcing reinforces the importance of public policies that allow workers to manage their best in a period of rapid economic change. This includes such things as ensuring the portability of health and pension benefits in order to reduce the adverse impact of changing jobs, which must inevitably happen in an ever-changing economy.

When a hand-wringing friend worried that some misfortunes would ruin the country, Adam Smith [1723–1790, economist and philosopher who wrote *An Inquiry into the Nature and Causes of the Wealth of Nations*] famously replied, "There is a great deal of ruin in a nation." The U.S. economy will face many challenges in coming decades, but as long as we do not stifle our dynamic economy that is the envy of the world, we need not fear that—as Mr. Roberts predicts—the U.S. will become a Third World nation by 2023.

6

Outsourcing Compromises the Safety and Quality of Products

Dali L. Yang

Dali L. Yang received his PhD in political science from Princeton University in New Jersey and is a professor at the University of Chicago in the Department of Political Science.

Concerns regarding the quality and safety of products manufactured in China have emerged as numerous products manufactured there have been recalled. The recalls revealed business practices in China that favor profit over safety and quality. In response, the Chinese government is taking steps to increase the quality and safety of products manufactured in China.

China once languished, a closed economy with several hundred million people living in abject poverty. Today [2008], it is a major engine for world economic growth. It boasts a rising middle class and the world's largest foreign-exchange reserves. There can no longer be talk about global trade without mentioning the dragon [China], and the American consumer would be hard-pressed to live without goods bearing the "Made in China" label.

For the past year [2007–2008], though, that very label has suffered from some serious image problems. Reports of toxic Chinese-made products have mushroomed: toys covered in

Dali L. Yang, "Total Recall," *The National Interest*, March/April 2008, pp. 42–49. Copyright © The National Interest 2008, Washington, D.C. Reproduced by permission.

lead paint, melamine-tainted pet food, defective tires, tooth-paste containing diethylene glycol, contaminated fish and more. There is also talk of unlicensed Chinese chemical companies eager to manufacture and supply fake, subpotent or adulterated drug products. To be sure, the bulk of Chinese exports to the United States are made or assembled to American specifications. Nonetheless, the lengthening list of unsafe goods from China also points to the simple fact that, in their quest for lower costs and higher profits, far too many China-based manufacturers are willing to cut corners at the expense of consumer safety.

Economic Growth Breeds Corruption

At their heart, China's real and exaggerated brand-image problems stem from a unique intersection of the American need for instant gratification and China's poisonous witches' brew of a "post-communist personality" with few moral moorings and an unfailing enthusiasm for getting rich. Too often now, the acquisitiveness so palpable in Chinese society knows no scruples, shifts the costs to others, and is married to opportunism and cunning. Of course, there are many businessmen who have made it big by working hard and honestly, but it's the anything-goes mind-set that rests at the root of many undesirable practices in China: from decadence to all manners of fake certificates, fake products, adulterated food and drinks, rampant official corruption and sheer disregard for the rights of workers in sweatshops. For many, socialism with Chinese characteristics has a lot in common with the early stage of capitalism Karl Marx described as primitive accumulation.

This phenomenon finds its roots in the Chinese brand of communism from which it was borne and the reforms from which it was shaped. Begun in the 1970s, the proliferation of unruly manufacturers and exporters in China sprang from an environment where the potential for entrepreneurship among peasants and tradesmen was stifled. Technicians were jailed for moonlighting as consultants, and collective farms were enthralled to the party-state. Private business activities were severely punished or suppressed.

But after years of oppression, the government began to allow market-oriented reforms to modernize China's economy. Within a decade, the forces of enterprise were unleashed, but hand in hand with growth came rampant corruption. Reform making and profit making have often meant getting ahead of official policies and bending and breaking existing laws and regulations.

Along with these market reforms came preferential treatment for those of "the Party." China's leaders (and especially Deng Xiaoping) opened the floodgates, allowing government and party agencies, the armed police and even the People's Liberation Army to supplement their budgets with profits that they generated on their own. Here we see the strange melding of the strong party-state that desired a profit with the willingness to bend the rules: government control and unruly capitalism. By the 1990s, the Chinese mentality was then fully transformed. Though the Tiananmen crackdown of 1989 [a pro-democracy movement of university students that was ended by military force] closed the route to political reforms, the raw energy unleashed in China was instead channeled to the pursuit of material wealth. Mammon [riches, material wealth] became the new religion. Business fever took over.

The amazingly quick turn from the asceticism of the Mao era to the cult of Mammon under the leadership of the same Communist Party has landed China in what author Xiaoying Wang termed "a moral wasteland." Indeed, this is the world of doublespeak, with everybody mouthing the rhetoric of the moment as dictated by the party and yet often doing exactly the opposite of what's prescribed. . . .

Product Safety and Quality

It is fitting that one of the most popular books in today's China, written by Li Zhongwu in 1912, highlights how thick skins and cunning were the ingredients for getting ahead in Chinese history.

The reality of this "personality" can be frightening, leading many manufacturers to search for loopholes to slip through to get a leg up due to the relentless pressure for cheaper products. Their goal is to make some quick money, using deceit if necessary. This was apparently the case for suppliers who provided lead paint to the ill-fated toy makers. Likewise, some Chinese suppliers of wheat gluten deliberately added melamine, an industrial chemical, to artificially boost their product's protein reading and thus grade and price. In this situation, Gresham's Law [which states that bad money drives good money out of circulation] prevails; honest firms find it hard to stay in business by competing on price. Even though a fix is available—manufacturers can lower costs and increase profits by improving the efficiency of production processes— oftentimes they just seek to substitute cheaper components. That can be done without sacrificing quality, but that often doesn't happen.

Product-quality and -safety cases are generally related to the continuing quest by manufacturers to lower production costs.

Yet, even with all this finger pointing, we have to keep in mind that the Chinese can't be blamed for all of the safety problems with products manufactured in-country. According to a Canadian analysis of data on toy recalls over the last twenty years, the majority of the recalls involving millions of toys manufactured in China were caused by design defects, with primary responsibility lying with the toy companies. Indeed, a Mattel executive recently admitted that the "vast majority of those products that were recalled were the result of a design flaw in Mattel's design, not through a manufacturing flaw in China's manufacturers." In such cases, the solution for the resultant safety problems needs to come from the (mostly U.S.) toy companies.

Unfortunately, the rest of the product-quality and -safety cases are generally related to the continuing quest by manufacturers to lower production costs in the face of distributors buying at low prices, a rising currency, and rising labor and raw-material costs. But this unbridled drive to profit, with all its market obstacles and ensuing corruption, has not escaped the Chinese government. Almost from the beginning, it was clear some reining-in was needed. So the contemporary history of economic growth and market expansion is also a history of the modern regulatory state. First steps were put in place—imperfect, but an encouraging start—and all hope for a "morally reformed" China is certainly not lost.

Building the Foundation

No fools they, in the early 1990s, the Chinese leadership took an initial stab at regulation after recognizing the need to build and rebuild the institutional infrastructure for a market economy. No modern economy allows the unbridled pursuit of self-interest, especially when that pursuit causes harm to others. In addition to the obvious internal problems, the collapse of communist regimes in the former Soviet Union and Eastern Europe and, later, the downfall of governments in South Korea and Indonesia during the Asian financial crisis spurred Beijing on even more. The Chinese leadership first reconfigured the tax and fiscal system to strengthen the central government's fiscal capabilities and then revamped the central banking system to enhance financial supervision and promote financial stability.

Of special significance was the divestiture program undertaken amid the Asian financial crisis. In one bold move, the

Chinese leadership got the People's Liberation Army, the armed police, the judiciary as well as a host of other party and state institutions out of the business of doing business. This divestiture helped bring rampant smuggling and related corruption under control and was critical to the development of a level economic playing field.

With the passage of time, China's leaders have also undertaken several rounds of government streamlining and restructuring to deal with an unruly market and rapidly changing socioeconomic conditions. In China, as in other developed nations, a bureaucratic alphabet soup of bodies has emerged to protect the rights of consumers, investors and workers. The advent of a consumer society and growing public awareness, in particular, have pushed safety and quality to the fore of policymaking. And happily, some of these institutions are becoming effective. . . .

While improved regulatory capability—up-to-date product standards, abilities to monitor, test and punish—is a necessity and can go a long way toward the mitigation of product-quality issues, it is generally less effective when dealing with rogue businesses whose intentions are to evade detection and make a quick buck. Shutting down a toxic plant after a scandal is one thing. Using bureaucracies for effective preventive measures is another.

While China has established various regulatory agencies, enforcement has not been optimal.

Cracks in the Mortar

The Chinese government realized that simply creating an array of institutions was not enough—the bureaucracy must also function well, something especially difficult to achieve in developing societies. From poor interagency cooperation to a lack of resources and sheer logistical difficulties, troubles remained. Herein lies the crux of the problem for regulators and consumers in the United States and elsewhere when it comes to the quality of products imported from abroad. While China has established various regulatory agencies, enforcement has not been optimal. Regulatory authority is now fragmented among a multitude of government agencies—each mindful of its own turf and interests—that often fail to work together, especially at the local levels. . . . Failure among the regulators to coordinate and cooperate with each other is believed to have contributed to the deadly milk-powder scandal that came to light in 2004 [when melamine was added to foods to make them appear to have a higher protein content].

Making matters worse, the interests between central and local authorities often diverge. In particular, lower-level authorities may be more tolerant of counterfeiters and other dishonest businesses in their jurisdictions simply because these businesses generate employment and tax revenue. In the words of a *Business Week* reporting team: "Even if Beijing has the best intentions of fixing problems such as undrinkable water and unbreathable air, it is often thwarted by hundreds of thousands of party officials with vested interests in the current system."

Partly to mitigate such divergence, the Chinese government has in recent years promoted the hierarchical integration of regulatory administrations, especially within the provinces. But, as pessimists argue, "China has built a bureaucratic machine that at times seems almost impervious to reform."

China's sheer scale and vast regional disparities present major challenges, too. While the major cities can deploy more personnel, resources and technology to enhance regulatory supervision, this is far from the case in outlying areas, where many of the small businesses, including counterfeiters, are often located.

Last but certainly not least, corruption has plagued some of the regulatory agencies, both in the headquarters and in the localities. Under Zheng Xiaoyu, the former head of the SFDA [State Food and Drug Administration], and his close associates, some pharmaceutical companies were able to obtain a large number of new drug approvals by submitting fake data and bribe money. Zheng was executed for bribe taking and dereliction of duty in 2007.

A history of Chinese regulatory developments in the reform era is thus one about the struggle to curb regulatory corruption and deal with and overcome various institutional flaws. As China's regulatory agencies contend with internal conflicts and cope with external pressures, are we sure they'll be able to effectively address their product-safety and -quality problems?. . .

Chinese officials openly express their annoyance at Western media reports they feel exaggerate the magnitude of China's product-safety problems.

Building Better

Sometimes a strong party-state is a very good thing. The successful corrective measures with respect to aviation safety and antidoping in international sports are undoubtedly encouraging. China is able to comply with international rules and norms. Recognizing that China's reputation was at stake, China's leaders took on serious reforms and tough regulatory actions. Unlike in many other developing countries, China, with its Communist Party, has the capacity to get things done when it matters.

Efforts to overcome corruption and cheating in the wake of opening up the Chinese market solved some problems, but created others. Though Chinese officials openly express their annoyance at Western media reports they feel exaggerate the magnitude of China's product-safety problems, they do realize that the reputation of "Made in China" is imperiled—and they care. As Vice Premier Wu Yi noted, bad press had caused "serious damage to China's national image." The government saw the writing on the wall and has taken a new wave of steps to improve watchdogging.

The United States and China have reached agreements to strengthen the quality of Chinese exports.

To help fix the problems plaguing regulatory agencies, like fragmentation and poor policy coordination, the State Council established a leading group on product quality and food safety in 2007. The leading group, headed by Vice Premier Wu Yi, is comprised of representatives from fifteen government agencies. And the Chinese government is putting muscle into policy implementation. Building on its long-standing efforts to improve market order, the Chinese government launched a nationwide campaign in August 2007 to investigate and fight the manufacture and sale of fake or substandard food, medicine and agricultural products. By October, the Chinese government had arrested 774 people in the crackdown. As of late November 2007, authorities had also closed down nearly eight thousand slaughterhouses for operating without licenses or for failing to meet government standards. For toy manufacturers blamed for producing toxic products, the Chinese government has suspended their export licenses—the kiss of death for an export business. Foshan Lee Der Toy Co., one of the first to be blamed for Mattel toys containing lead, was shut down. The owner committed suicide.

But most importantly, the Chinese are upgrading quality standards in all areas, from food to pharmaceuticals. They're taking proactive measures to strengthen the monitoring and supervision of production and supply chains for food and manufactures, including implementing monitoring and inspection programs for wholesale farm-produce markets in all major cities, introducing recall mechanisms for food and more rigorously testing the quality of export products at the border.

In spite of the domestic campaign and crackdown, it is simply impossible for Chinese regulators to achieve full compliance in the domestic market in a short time period. There are hundreds of thousands of firms and families involved in producing food and manufactures. So, the focus of governmental action is, in the words of Wu Yi, "to strengthen the system of supervision and control over product quality, especially relating to *exports*." This means that, while there will be general improvement, the improvement in the domestic market will likely lag behind that of exports.

International Expectations

As with aviation-safety regulation and antidoping, the international pressure on China to improve product quality has been accompanied by international assistance. We can hope this collaboration will be as effective. On products ranging from preserved and pet foods and farm-raised fish to certain drugs, medical devices and toys, the United States and China have reached agreements to strengthen the quality of Chinese exports. Whereas previously, authorities would ignore the errant or unlicensed factories until after a product-quality problem had been uncovered, the agreements signed during the Third U.S.-China Strategic Economic Dialogue in December 2007 require Chinese exporters to register with the government and accept inspections to ensure compliance with American standards. This is clearly designed to mitigate counterfeiting and safety problems before the products even leave China.

Also as part of the agreements, and as an indication of the growing interdependence between the Chinese and American economies, Beijing has allowed U.S. inspectors to become "embedded" in China to monitor the quality standards of certain Chinese export products, ensuring they meet U.S. quality standards. Stationing U.S. FDA [Food and Drug Administration] personnel abroad helps bridge different regulatory systems. This kind of cooperation is a nascent but significant step toward deep regulatory integration and may also be replicated in other countries. All this highlights the disparity between American and developing-world standards.

Western buyers, mindful of the high costs of safety-related recalls, have become more demanding when it comes to quality and safety.

Meanwhile, even without the major Chinese government initiatives, the massive recalls would have caused businesses on both sides of the Pacific to modify their behavior. Western buyers, mindful of the high costs of safety-related recalls, have become more demanding when it comes to quality and safety. On the other side, many Chinese manufacturers quickly adopted more rigorous testing and tightened quality standards to keep the orders coming in. Those unable to bear the rising costs and risks have simply exited the market.

It's unlikely that government regulation will be fully effective in the Chinese domestic market, if for no other reason than the sheer number of businesses that need to be regulated. But when it comes to Chinese exports to developed markets, the message is clear: Beijing will ensure products destined for American markets meet U.S. standards. As Wu Yi said, "China will live up to its responsibilities and obligations when it comes to product quality and food safety." Both government initiatives and market forces will point the way. After all, China's reputation is at stake.

7

The Majority of Americans Believe Free Trade Is Hampering the U.S. Economy

Nina Easton

Nina Easton frequently appears on the Fox News Channel as a commentator and serves as the Washington, D.C., bureau chief for Fortune *magazine.*

Americans are concerned about the effects of free trade on the economy. The enactment of the North American Free Trade Agreement has caused workers to lose jobs as factories close. Solutions include training U.S. workers for jobs that cannot be outsourced to other countries, halting imports from countries that use child labor, limiting imports from countries that pollute the environment, and encouraging product ingenuity to compete in a global economy.

"We are the champions—of the world" may be the verse that rings out in stadiums across the U.S., but in the great game of global trade, Americans are increasingly feeling like the losers. A large majority—68%—of those surveyed in a new *Fortune* poll says America's trading partners are benefiting the most from free trade, not the U.S. That sense of victimhood is changing America's attitude about doing business with the world.

We are a nation crawling into a fetal position, cramped by fear that America has lost control of its destiny in a fiercely competitive global economy. The fear is mostly about jobs lost overseas and wages capped by foreign competition.

But it is also fueled by lead-painted toys from China and border-hopping workers from Mexico, by the housing and credit crisis at home [in 2008], and by the residue of vulnerability left by 9/11 and the wars that followed. Americans were willing to experiment with open borders during the exuberant 1990s. Today that mood has darkened. We are turning inward. Especially now, as the U.S. economy sputters, we are on the verge of becoming a country of economic nationalists.

That may be hard to imagine if you are reading these words from the aisle seat of a packed business-class cabin on one of those new nonstop flights to Guangzhou or Mumbai or Abu Dhabi, the numbers on your company's latest deal flashing on your laptop screen. It may be hard to imagine, too, if your factory can't keep up with orders for diesel engines flooding in from Beijing or electronic parts requests from Brazil. Despite a continued massive trade imbalance, U.S. exports grew 12% last year [2007], providing a cushion against the painful housing downturn.

Americans have increasingly felt that they're running in place. Median household income in 2006 . . . was barely ahead of where it was eight years earlier.

Free Trade and the Middle Class

Yet for several years average Americans have increasingly felt that they're running in place. Median household income in 2006, at $48,201, was barely ahead of where it was eight years earlier. So the prospect of a recession has made the anxious middle class even more so. Coming in [the 2008] presidential election season, the approaching storm clouds have turned the economy into the No. 1 issue on the campaign trail. Fear is a potent force in American politics, and Democratic Party leaders have astutely tapped into rising voter unease about globalization.

Fortune's poll, a survey of 1,000 adult Americans taken Jan. 14–16, shows that voters have identified winners and losers in the free-trade agenda. Nearly half of those polled believe that growth in international trade has made things better for consumers (though nearly as many think it has made things worse), but 55% believe American business has been harmed, and 78% think it has made things worse for American workers.

As many as 40 million U.S. jobs could be vulnerable, thanks to modern technology and more than one billion eligible new workers.

North American Free Trade Agreement

Candidate Barack Obama encapsulated this feeling on the campaign trail in December [2007] when he said, "People don't want a cheaper T-shirt if they're losing a job in the process." What might be dismissed as just campaign-season populism has been given intellectual credibility by some economists, notably Princeton's Alan Blinder, a professed free-trader who has crossed over into the camp of those concerned about the outsourcing of service industry work. He has predicted that as many as 40 million U.S. jobs could be vulnerable, thanks to modern technology and more than one billion eligible new workers.

Speaking in November at a Federal Reserve Bank of Chicago conference, he declared, "It's not the British that are coming. It's the electrons that are coming, and it's going to cost jobs." The national mood swing is a dramatic one. With stubborn optimism and entrepreneurial swagger, Americans led the world in building a roadmap for global commerce during the 1990s, when Bill Clinton overcame resistance from organized labor to sign the North American Free Trade Agreement (NAFTA), linking the U.S., Canada, and Mexico to create the world's largest trade bloc.

It was an internal party battle that Clinton took on with gusto, beginning in the fall of 1991, when as a presidential candidate he shut down a debate among his strategists over what position he should take on trade. "Finally, Clinton looked up over his spectacles and said, 'I want all of you to understand something: I'm not going to run as an isolationist, and I'm not going to run as a protectionist,'" recalls William Galston, a party strategist now at the Brookings Institution. "I'll never forget that day."

President Clinton was able to bring along a majority of the public on an aggressive free-trade agenda. But today, according to the *Fortune* poll, nearly two-thirds of Americans are even willing to pay higher prices to keep down foreign competition. Now Clinton's party is leading America into this new era of doubt, its economic gurus convinced that globalization—in its current form—is costing the middle class and enriching an elite.

A Time-out for Free Trade

Both Democratic frontrunners [in the 2008 presidential election] want changes to NAFTA, which Hillary Clinton now says has "serious shortcomings." . . . Obama praises globalization for bringing millions of workers into the global economy but wants a tax code that discourages companies from shipping jobs overseas.

No matter which candidate or which party takes control of the White House one year from now [in 2009], free trade will—in the words of Hillary Clinton—take a "time-out." That's because Congress—which will most likely remain in the hands of the Democrats regardless of who wins the White House in November—took away President [George W.] Bush's ability to negotiate trade deals by quietly letting so-called fast-track authority lapse last summer. And lawmakers won't hand that power back to any new President—Democrat or Republican—without major new federal programs (and new trade rules) designed to ease the stress of globalization on U.S. workers.

The Democratic mantra is now "fair trade, not free trade." During a "time-out" on trade deals, a President Obama or President Clinton would seek to extend international labor and environmental standards (already approved by Bush in the current crop of deals) and step up enforcement against China and other trading partners. A Republican President will need to accede to most of those demands to move a trade agenda forward in a Democrat-controlled Congress, and at least one of the party's leading presidential candidates—former Arkansas governor Mike Huckabee—is mostly in sync with the Democratic mood, complaining about "an unlevel, unfair trading arena that has to be fixed."

It's not just America that's experiencing a trade backlash. Peter Mandelson, the European Union's commissioner for trade, looks past his frustrating meetings with free-trade skeptics on Capitol Hill to his own continent and describes growing "economic insecurity that is ripe for disaster, that feeds populism and protectionism." Former U.S. Trade Representative Mickey Kantor told *Fortune* that as the global economy becomes more integrated, "trade has lost more and more credibility all around the world—India, Brazil, France. For some reason, everyone thinks they are the loser."

Maytag as a Metaphor

In the U.S. the newly shuttered Maytag plant in Newton, Iowa, doubles as an altar to the political spirit of economic nationalism. In the months leading up to the Iowa caucuses, Democratic candidates—and Republican Huckabee—trooped into town to . . . borrow its brick image for their argument that globalization has hurt the middle class and enriched a narrow elite on Wall Street. Maytag, which anchored this town for more than a century before it was battered by foreign competition, seemed the perfect election-year symbol for the price of globalization.

But was U.S. trade policy really the culprit? "Maytag was mismanaged," says town mayor Charles Allen. By the time rival Whirlpool gobbled it up in 2006, Maytag's market share was at an all-time low, customers were grumbling about the quality of its washers and dryers, and one analyst was quoted describing the company as a "two-inch putt from bankruptcy." Maytag CEO Ralph Hake was blamed for cost cutting that destroyed innovation.

When I visited Newton on the eve of the Iowa caucuses, I expected a dying town. Instead I found a vibrant community of 16,000 with serene neighborhoods and a bustling downtown. The damage caused by the plant's closure shouldn't be minimized—unemployment in the area shot up to 5.6%, far above the state average. But Allen says the town had long been adjusting to the prospect of losing its largest employer. A NASCAR raceway has opened; a new biodiesel plant is up and running; TPI Composites, a wind turbine manufacturer with plants in Mexico and China, has just agreed to build a new facility with 500 jobs. And about 50 former Maytag engineers have launched their own research and development business, called Springboard.

Public Response to Free Trade

All this local ingenuity and determination to create a new economy was lost in the political noise leading up to the Iowa caucuses. Most analysts agree that the underlying reason for public anxiety over globalization is the visibility of factory closings and the stagnation of income. But the reasons behind this decline are complex. Technology, for one. "It's first and foremost a story of technology and of the technology driving out middle-income jobs—whether they are in services or in manufacturing," economist Laura D'Andrea Tyson, an advisor to Hillary Clinton, told *Fortune's* Global Forum [in October 2007]. By contrast, for educated elites "technology gives you a global stage on which to earn your income."

Diana Farrell, director of the McKinsey Global Institute [an economics research group], cites demographics for a "very large part of the softening in growth of wages." In other words, wages moved upward with a baby-boom generation that saw rising waves of Americans going to college and then on to higher-paying jobs. But that upward motion has crested; the population has stabilized. But those aren't answers that satisfy voters in a heated election campaign. (As Tyson noted, "On the campaign trail, a one-sentence answer is what matters.")

[Seventy-nine percent] of those surveyed said the U.S. government hasn't done enough to help workers who lose their jobs to foreign competition.

So Democratic leaders have tapped into the sour public mood over globalization. "The public is not listening for how you expand trade," says Kantor, a Democratic veteran now informally advising Hillary Clinton. "The public wants to hear just how frightened you are. Someone has to say, 'I understand it, I get it.'" But then what?

Most Democratic leaders insist they don't want to, nor believe they can, halt the global flow of commerce. Where they hope to connect with voters is by promising to strengthen the safety net. "America frankly does a disgraceful job with displaced workers," declares economist Blinder. Americans resoundingly agree: In our poll, 79% of those surveyed said the U.S. government hasn't done enough to help workers who lose their jobs to foreign competition.

People in the survey favor more job training, longer unemployment benefits, and limits on imports from countries that use child labor or pollute the environment. Blinder calls for an education system more focused on jobs that can't be shipped offshore. There are plenty of worthy ideas, but policy prescriptions have to be combined with leadership that encourages Americans once again to believe in their ability to compete in the world. Just as the shutdown Maytag factory provided an easy symbol of globalization's cost in the 2008 election, the town of Newton, Iowa, could symbolize the ultimate gains of adjustment in the next. But only because of a belief by local leaders that they wanted to be part of a global economy, not shut off from it.

8

America Has Prospered from Outsourcing So Protectionism Is Not Needed

Milton Ezrati

Milton Ezrati is a senior economic strategist at investment management firm Lord, Abbett & Co. Prior to joining Lord Abbett, Ezrati was a senior vice president at Nomura Asset Management.

Foreign competition is nothing new. Over the past fifty years, the United States has encountered stiff competition from countries such as Germany, Japan, and Mexico. The United States overcame these obstacles from foreign competition through innovation.

Although the media for the time being has shed its panic over the outsourcing of jobs abroad, the issue nonetheless remains dangerous, not to American jobs directly, that was always overblown, but because the fear of outsourcing presents a powerful and ongoing political temptation to protectionism [policy of imposing limitations on imports to protect domestic industries from overseas competition]. . . . The stakes are high. Even a hint that the United States might withdraw support for the world's free-trade regime (painstakingly developed during past decades) threatens global growth prospects and consequently more American jobs than any Chinese toy

Milton Ezrati, "Misplaced Fears: Why the Outsourcing Scare Is Overblown," *The International Economy*, Fall 2004, pp. 79–81. Reproduced by permission.

factory or Indian call center could. It is critically important, then, to put this situation into perspective.

The issue of outsourcing overseas is neither new nor is it as overwhelming as some suggest. At base, it is just the latest installment in the long-standing challenge to the United States from cheap foreign labor, one that began in the 1950s, when European wages were low, and has continued over time with a shifting focus to various countries. Since it is not new, it does not require new solutions, especially a dangerous protectionist response. The United States has managed throughout this long time without resorting to protectionism. It has instead met the challenge of cheap foreign labor successfully with impressive gains in labor productivity and ongoing innovation. The country can do the same in the present instance, too.

Foreign Wages vs. Domestic Wages

There can be little doubt that today's challenge from low foreign wages is as great as it has ever been. A few simple comparisons illustrate. According to IBM, a Chinese programmer with three to five years of experience earns the equivalent of around $12.50 an hour. His American equivalent makes closer to $56.00 an hour. American firms operating in Bangalore, India, note that a software engineer there makes about $30,000 year, less than one-sixth of his Silicon Valley equivalent. The average English-speaking telephone operator in India makes about $1.50 an hour, compared with $11.00 for a similar operator in the States.

Such vast wage differences seem insurmountable and lead naturally to frightening views of a future full of unemployment and poverty. Feeding that fear is a report from the Gartner Group, an independent consulting firm. It indicates that some 80 percent of American boards of directors have responded to such wage differentials by discussing outsourcing offshore. More than 40 percent have completed some sort of a pilot project. Forrester Research, another private consulting group, estimates that this country will export a total of 3.3 million white-collar jobs by 2015, including 1.7 million back office jobs and 473,000 positions in information technology. The [U.S.] Department of Commerce has extrapolated recent trends in outsourcing and estimated that service imports of legal work, computer programming, telecommunications, banking, engineering, and management consulting will rise rapidly from [the 2003] level of about $17.4 billion to erase the country's trade surplus in services in just a few years.

For more than half a century, wage differentials between the United States and some foreign rival have always seemed insurmountable, at least at first.

Foreign Competition Anxiety

But such frightening projections are nothing new. For more than half a century, wage differentials between the United States and some foreign rival have always seemed insurmountable, at least at first, and people have feared the worst. In the 1950s and 1960s, financial journalists and politicians fretted that the country would lose all its manufacturing to low-wage German labor. It is hard today to think of German labor as cheap, but it was back then. After the European scare, there was Japan, with automobiles in the 1970s and more generally in the 1980s. It, too, occasioned dire predictions. Then it was Mexico and now China and India. At each phase, of course, ongoing changes in technology and the economies of the world rendered different jobs vulnerable. The particular institutional arrangements altered, too. With Europe and Japan, the competition came mostly from foreign firms, whereas more recently, it has come from American firms subcontracting to their own foreign subsidiaries. But at base, the story has consistently been one of low-cost foreign labor.

At each phase during this long period, the forecasts of disaster sound remarkably like today's doomsaying. John

Kennedy, for example, in his 1960 presidential campaign, spoke of foreign competition carrying "the dark menace of industrial dislocation, increasing unemployment, and deepening poverty." Twenty years later, when the threat came from Japan, prominent financier Felix Rohatyn talked about "deindustrialization" and the prospect of America becoming "a nation of short-order cooks and saleswomen." At that same time, then-Senator Lloyd Bentsen (D-TX) worried: "American workers will end up like the people in the biblical village who were condemned to be hewers of wood and drawers of water." A short while later, Walter Mondale, while serving as U.S. ambassador to Japan, suggested that Americans would soon be fit only to sweep the floors in Japanese factories. By the late 1980s, when Japan was beginning to fall into stagnation and the foreign threat had shifted to Mexico, then presidential candidate Ross Perot could hear the "giant sucking sound" of lost jobs. On the verge of the great technological leap of the 1990s, a Pulitzer Prize went to two journalists, Donald L. Barlett and James B. Steele, for their book on America's decline, *America: What Went Wrong.*

The country has coped through technological innovation and product development to create new jobs for otherwise displaced workers.

Almost all these ugly outlooks have come equipped with calls for protectionist measures. Fortunately, the nation has resisted this misguided political solution. The United States instead has coped by applying its genius for productivity enhancement. Ever-higher levels of productivity allowed American workers to warrant their relatively high wages, even if it meant fewer workers on a given project. And the country has coped through technological innovation and product development to create new jobs for otherwise displaced workers in new and previously unimagined industries and pursuits.

Technology and Jobs

The stress on productivity probably would have occurred even without foreign competition. American producers would still have responded to this country's high wages with robotics and other labor-saving techniques. Their efforts would still have raised the productivity of some workers and forced layoffs on others. Receptionists, after all, have faced a similar experience from the introduction of voice mail, even though foreign competition has hardly applied to them. The same could be said for bank tellers and ATM machines. Middle management has faced the same from improved systems and communications, even in those areas where foreign competition is not an issue. Some of the jobs lost to automation and systems have, of course, reappeared overseas, not because they were stolen, but rather because the low wages abroad relieve those operations of any need for labor saving techniques. Either way, high-paid American labor has lost the jobs.

With innovation and productivity growth, the United States . . . has become more prosperous.

Innovation Creates New Opportunities

Those displaced by heightened productivity, whether inspired by foreign competition or not, have suffered until ultimately innovation created new industries with new employment opportunities. Throughout the transition, of course, people have doubted that the new industries and new jobs would develop. That is understandable, since at any point in time it is difficult to envision where innovation will take the economy. In the 1950s and 1960s, for instance, when cheap European labor threatened America's traditional steel industry, few could imagine how the telecommunications and technological revolutions of the last forty years would employ millions in previously undreamed of jobs. In the 1970s and 1980s, when

Japanese competition threatened employment in the auto industry and some of the new areas of technology, people could not see how innovation in this country would create a separate revolution in finance that transformed an industry dominated by bank clerks into one that employs millions at all levels, many in high-paying advisory positions that did not exist even twenty years ago. Similarly, cable and direct television have made their own employment revolution, creating jobs for millions at all skill and pay levels from technicians to executives. These are only the most obvious illustrations of the opportunities that have absorbed many of those displaced from more traditional industries for whatever reason.

With this innovation and productivity growth, the United States has put the lie to those ongoing forecasts of unemployment and poverty. Instead, the country has become more prosperous. In the past twenty years, for example, the growth of the information economy has created an 80 percent increase in management positions from 23.6 million in the early 1980s to 42.5 million today. The proportion of such challenging, high-paying jobs has risen from 23.4 percent of the workforce to 31.1 percent. Testifying even more broadly to the effectiveness of productivity growth and innovation, the nation's standard of living has risen throughout this time, and impressively so. According to the Commerce Department's Bureau of Economic Analysis, per capita income [in 2003] averaged $28,215, up 175 percent in real terms from 1960, 58 percent from 1980, and almost 20 percent even from the boom year 1996. Clearly, most workers, if not every one, are doing better than they once were, despite the foreign competition.

Outlook of the Future

For all the opportunity, there is no denying that the transitions forced by these patterns have also imposed great hardship on groups of workers and regions of the country. These deserve attention. But it is misguided to extrapolate such hardship to make endless warnings of general economic collapse and call for protectionist measures, especially in the face of the remarkably successful historic record. Looking forward, there is, of course, always the risk that the solutions of the past will fail, that the productivity growth will falter or the innovation fade. But the prospects of such a radical departure from past trends is not especially likely. Even though few today have the clairvoyance to paint a definite picture of future innovations and the new job opportunities, the long record of the past certainly raises the odds that they will occur and that the country will cope without the need to resort to protectionism.

9

Outsourcing Is a Precursor to Foreign Investors Obtaining U.S. Infrastructure

William Norman Grigg

William Norman Grigg served as a senior editor of the New American *magazine and authored* America's Engineered Decline.

Products manufactured in China and purchased by American consumers weaken the U.S. economy. The United States' deficit and dependence on goods made in China are placing the Chinese in a position of power over the United States. The Chinese are stockpiling billions of dollars that could be used to purchase tangible property within the United States, such as roads and bridges.

We begin with a parable: Driven to the streets after a run of relentless misfortune, a man took up station on a street corner holding a hand-lettered sign stating: "Will work for food."

Most pedestrians and motorists passed the desperate man without so much as a second's worth of thought. One exception was a well-dressed businessman, who read the sign while waiting for the street light to change. But burdened by thoughts of his own concerns, the businessman gave in to a moment of imprudent sarcasm.

William Norman Grigg, "Buyout of America," *The New American*, September 4, 2006, p. 12(6). Copyright © 2006 American Opinion Publishing Incorporated. Reproduced by permission.

"You 'work for food'? I work for Visa!" he exclaimed to the sign-bearing man. "I'm working for food I ate years ago!" After getting the green light, the businessman launched one last unworthy gibe:

"You're not broke—you're even!"

The homeless man eventually found a steady job paying just enough for him to get by and save a little money. His employer, a large and amoral conglomerate paying most of its employees subsistence wages, used its workers' savings (which the conglomerate controls) to make loans to spendthrifts' like the heavily leveraged businessman—people who continued to live well beyond their means by stretching their credit lines well past the breaking point. At the same time, the conglomerate quietly used its expanding financial holdings to buy up practically everything in sight.

Eventually, the loans were called in, the debtors were unable to pay, and the businessman found himself—along with many of his fellow spendthrifts—working for that same predatory conglomerate. His earnings and standard of living were "harmonized downward" to those of the homeless man whose plight he had once mocked.

A Realistic Appraisal

Adapted from a stand-up routine broadcast on Comedy Central about a decade ago, this parable is not intended to inspire mockery of the homeless or other unfortunate people. It's intended to encourage a realistic appraisal of our national economic condition [in 2006]. Think of the homeless man as symbolizing the poor but industrious Chinese population, willing and eager to work for a fraction of what Americans earn, and the businessman as a stand-in for an American population whose prosperity is largely a debt-enhanced illusion.

The conglomerate, of course, is the entity upon which our nation and our government have become increasingly dependent to underwrite that pseudo-prosperity: the communist Chinese regime, which is rapidly acquiring the means quite literally to buy our country out from underneath us.

Indeed, the process of selling off public assets to foreign interests is already underway.

In June [2006], for example, a Spanish-Australian conglomerate paid $3.8 billion to lease the Indiana Toll Road. Transfer of electronic tolling equipment began in August, and by fall it is expected that the new foreign owners will be collecting tolls once paid by Indiana residents to their own state government. And similar deals are being struck by states and municipalities across the country.

"Roads and bridges built by U.S. taxpayers are starting to be sold off, and so far foreign-owned companies are doing the buying," reported the Associated Press [AP]. At present the main foreign players in these deals are companies based in Australia and Spain. But as China accumulates ever-increasing quantities of depreciating dollars, it will start looking for tangible goods in which to invest those dollars. And as we will see, some analysts in this country are suggesting that we should welcome Chinese "direct investment" in our country as a way of closing our imponderably huge "fiscal gap."

At some point, perhaps very soon, Beijing will have the ability to decimate our currency by selling off its dollar-denominated bonds.

Beijing Buyout

"Without Chinese support, the dollar would have already collapsed, bond yields would have soared, and the U.S. economy would already be in a recession, if not a depression," observe Bill Bonner and Addison Wiggin in their study *Empire of Debt: The Rise of an Epic Financial Crisis*. "Where does the money come from? The Chinese get the dead presidents from selling products to live Americans, who seem ready to consume anything that comes their way. First, the dollars come rolling off U.S. printing presses, then they make their way into the hands of Chinese and other manufacturers, and finally, they are returned to their birthplace as loans. China is fast becoming America's 'company store,' to whom we owe our standard of living and maybe even our soul."

By accumulating hundreds of billions of dollars in their foreign-exchange holdings, the Chinese are acquiring the power to define our nation's economic destiny. At some point, perhaps very soon, Beijing will have the ability to decimate our currency by selling off its dollar-denominated bonds. But this would inflict severe damage on China's economy as well, making that option the economic equivalent of a suicide-bomb attack.

The federal government keeps two sets of books.

A better approach, from Beijing's perspective, would be to take its huge and expanding supply of depreciating dollars and invest them in tangible productive assets. In recent years, China has been following that approach in the Western Hemisphere. During his 2005 tour of Latin America, President Hu Jintao inked lucrative energy and resource deals with Brazil, Argentina, and Venezuela. In January [2006], China completed a deal with Canada for joint development of Alberta's uranium mines and oil sands.

With Beijing using its dollar hoard to buy up assets in both South America and Canada, what's to stop it from buying up the U.S.A.—a debt-plagued country with vast natural resources, the world's best transportation system, and a huge (and increasingly idle) manufacturing base?

Horrifying as the prospect of a Beijing buyout would be to most Americans, the concept is being discussed, in principle, by some policymakers as a solution to our impending—and all but inevitable national bankruptcy.

"The federal government keeps two sets of books," noted *USA Today* for August 3 [2006]. "The set the government promotes to the public has a healthier bottom line: a $318 billion deficit in 2005." An "audited financial statement produced by the government's accountants following standard accounting rules discloses that the actual deficit for 2005 was $760 billion," continues the paper. And if the costs of Social Security and Medicare were included in the total, as any honest accounting would require, "the federal deficit would have been $3.5 trillion."

That's the annual deficit—not the national debt. In what sense is a deficit of nearly one-third of a trillion dollars "healthy"? In roughly the same sense that congestive heart failure is "healthier" than a sucking chest wound: Both are lethal if untreated, but the latter will kill much more quickly.

"We're a bottom-line culture, and we've been hiding the bottom line from the American people," complains Rep. Jim Cooper (D-Tenn.), a former investment banker who offered a draft resolution—supported by congressmen on both sides of the aisle—to require the president to include audited spending and deficit numbers in his budget proposals. "It's not fair to [the people], and it's delusional on our part." That Washington has invested heavily in the preservation of that delusional system is illustrated by the fact that Rep. Cooper's proposal for honest accounting wasn't even considered by the Senate.

Official Washington remains determined to conceal the size of the "fiscal gap"—a figure that includes not only the existing national debt, but also future commitments, such as Medicare and Social Security. A 2005 report compiled for the National Bureau of Economic Research by economists Jagadeesh Gokhale and Kent Smetters concluded that the fiscal gap is $65.9 trillion, and growing.

Headed for Bankruptcy

The "fiscal gap," explains Professor Laurence J. Kotlikoff of Boston University, offers the most telling measure of a country's solvency. If the "fiscal burdens facing current and future generations . . . exceed the resources of those generations, get close to doing so or simply get so high as to preclude their full collection, the country's policy will be unsustainable and can constitute or lead to national bankruptcy."

By any rational reckoning, the United States has already reached that point.

The estimated fiscal gap of $65.9 trillion "is more than five times U.S. GDP [gross domestic product] and almost twice the size of national wealth," Kotlikoff continues. "One way to wrap one's head around $65.9 trillion is to ask what fiscal adjustments are needed to eliminate this red hole. The answers are terrifying. One solution is an immediate and permanent doubling of personal and corporate income taxes. Another is an immediate and permanent two-thirds cut in Social Security and Medicare benefits. A third alternative, were it feasible, would be to immediately and permanently cut all federal discretionary spending [optional government spending] by 143 percent."

Beijing as "Savior"?!

These details are offered by Dr. Kotlikoff in "Is the United States Bankrupt?" a . . . paper commissioned by the Federal Reserve Bank of St. Louis. To begin closing the fiscal gap, Kotlikoff urges imposition of a national sales tax to replace existing income, payroll, and estate taxes; phasing out the existing Social Security Program in favor of a Personal Security System into which all workers would be required to give 7.15 percent of their wages into an investment fund managed by the Social Security Administration; and abolishing Medicare and Medicaid in favor of a "Medical Security System," under which

Americans would receive "an individual-specific voucher to be used to purchase health insurance for the following calendar year."

Kotlikoff believes that these radical reforms would dramatically reduce the level of current federal spending—which is, at best, a debatable assumption. In any case, a fiscal gap still remains that can only be closed through additional revenues. How is it to be overcome?

Some relatively optimistic commentators insist that increased productivity—working smarter, rather than harder—will lead to consistent growth in the U.S. Gross Domestic Product. Kotlikoff, after crunching the numbers, doesn't buy into this assessment.

Unlikely as it may seem that foreign interests could buy our country out from beneath us, the process is already underway.

"Were productivity growth a certain cure for the nation's fiscal problems, the cure would already have occurred," Kotlikoff points out. "Assuming the United States could restrain the growth in its expenditures—is there a reliable source of productivity improvement to be tapped? The answer is yes, and the answer lies with China."

"Not only is China supplying capital to the rest of the world, it's increasingly doing so via direct investment," he points out. "For example, China is investing large sums in Iran, Africa, and Eastern Europe." Given that China holds hundreds of billions of dollars in its foreign exchange reserve, the question for the United States "is whether China will tire of investing only indirectly in our country and begin to sell its dollar-denominated reserves. Doing so could have spectacularly bad implications for the value of the dollar and the level of U.S. interest rates."

Another possibility presents itself, however: China could use its dollar hoard to buy valuable assets within the United States. In other words, rather than dumping its dollars, China could use them to buy up the United States.

"Fear of Chinese investment in the United States seems terribly misplaced," Kotlikoff writes soothingly. "With a national saving rate running at only 2.1 percent—a postwar [i.e., since World War II] low—the United States desperately needs foreigners to invest in the country. And the country with the greatest potential for doing so going forward is China." In fact, China could emerge as "the world's saver and, thereby, the developed world's savior with respect to its long-run supply of capital."

The Buyout Begins

Unlikely as it may seem that foreign interests could buy our country out from beneath us, the process is already underway.

"On a single day in June," reported the AP on July 15, [2006,] "an Australian-Spanish partnership paid $3.8 billion to lease the Indiana Toll Road. An Australian company bought a 99-year lease on Virginia's Pocahontas Parkway, and Texas officials decided to let a Spanish-American partnership build and run a toll road from Austin to Seguin for 50 years. Few people know that the tolls from the U.S. side of the tunnel between Detroit and Windsor, Canada, go to a subsidiary of an Australian company—which also owns a bridge in Alabama." These are just a few examples of how roads and bridges built with U.S. taxpayer dollars are starting to be sold off, and so far foreign-owned companies are doing the buying.

State and local governments are strapped for cash and relatively limited in the financial tools at their disposal. (While they can float bond issues, for instance, they cannot simply write blank checks that are covered by new money printed by the Federal Reserve.) Thus many of them, lured by the prospect of a quick influx amounting to billions of dollars, have put public assets—highways, airports, utilities, and even state-run lotteries—on the auction block.

The Worst of Both Worlds

While this approach offers a short-term remedy for state and local governments, it leaves the public facing the worst of both worlds: the prospect of increased taxes to cover rising local expenses, plus paying fees and tolls to foreign companies that are, in effect, absentee landlords over what had been locally controlled infrastructure. Referring to the sale of a 75-year lease over the Indiana Toll Road to an Australian-Spanish consortium, Democratic state Representative Patrick Bauer summarized the lose–lose proposition: "In five, maybe 10 years, all that money is gone, and the tolls keep rising and the money keeps flowing into the foreign coffers."

Last winter [February 2006], much of the United States was figuratively up in arms over the prospect of an executive branch deal to permit Dubai, one of the United Arab Emirates (UAE), to operate U.S. port facilities. This was seen, with just reason, as a potentially disastrous breach of national security, since it would put our port security in the hands of a company owned by a government cozy with al-Qaeda. Yet less than six months later, Congress enacted a "free-trade" agreement with Oman—which borders Yemen, Saudi Arabia, and the UAE—that would permit government-controlled companies in that Arab nation to own and operate U.S. ports.

Not surprisingly, China—which now controls the most crucial port facilities in the hemisphere, the "anchor ports" to the Panama Canal—is looking to build on that advantage, and it has cash-hungry politicians across the country lining up to help.

In late July [2006], three members of the Dallas City Council—Ed Oakley, Bill Blaydes, and Ron Natinsky—traveled to China to discuss a possible joint venture involving building and operating a shipping, storage, and distribution facility located inland for the purpose of relieving congestion at seaside entry ports, called the "Inland Port of Dallas," described by *Traffic World* as the "linchpin of a new NAFTA corridor." (The nascent Dallas port facility already has a working relationship with the Chinese-controlled Panama Canal Authority.) "Dallas hopes to become the place where East meets West—literally," notes the publication. "It seeks Asian imports in containers shipped from Los Angeles and Long Beach and intermodal freight moving north from Mexico on the proposed $180 billion Trans-Texas Corridor, or 'TTC.'"

[Several American cities] hope to use transportation and logistics assets to become the next big North American Gateway for Asian imports.

This explains the pilgrimage of Dallas councilmen to Beijing to court China's favor. Houston's city government has also made a pitch to China. Both Houston and Corpus Christi are reportedly offering Beijing access to ports on the Gulf of Mexico, and China is reportedly in negotiations to lease Kelly Air Force Base, which was converted into an industrial park about five years ago.

But these developments in Texas are just "part of a larger battle that involves cities such as Kansas City, Missouri; St. Louis; Memphis, Tennessee; and even Indianapolis, all of which hope to use transportation and logistics assets to become the next big North American Gateway for Asian imports," concludes *Traffic World*.

Beijing, U.S.A.

But we're not just talking about importing inexpensive Chinese-made consumer goods. Remember the process described by [William] Bonner and [Addison] Wiggin in *Empire of Debt*: dollars are printed by the Federal Reserve, which are spent on Chinese-made goods, and end up being sent back to the United States as loans, which are used to buy more Chinese-made goods.

We've reached the point in this process where American politicians are literally begging Beijing to be taken on as business partners. And if Laurence Kotlikoff's recommendations prove attractive to policymakers, our government will come to embrace "direct investment" from China as the key to staving off utter insolvency.

What this could mean, in practical terms, is that the debt-wracked American middle class would suffer the fate of the businessman in our parable.

10

Multinational Corporations Can Benefit the Economy During a Recession

Michael Mandel, Steve Hamm, and Christopher Ferrell

Michael Mandel is the chief economist for BusinessWeek *magazine and holds a PhD in economics from Harvard University. Steve Hamm is a senior writer at* BusinessWeek *and has a bachelor of arts from Carnegie Mellon University. Christopher Ferrell is a contributing editor for* BusinessWeek *and is a graduate of Stanford University and the London School of Economics and Political Science.*

As credit lines tighten for domestic corporations, multinational corporations are recording soaring profits from operations overseas. Multinational corporations are known for being well-managed, productive, and high-wage firms. Economists are taking notice and are looking at the positive impact multinational corporations can have on the U.S. economy during a recession.

High in the hills overlooking Corning, N.Y., the company named after the town has recently broken ground on a $300 million expansion of its research laboratories. Flush with cash from booming overseas sales, the glass giant is amping up its product development efforts at home. "It's important for the functioning of our innovation machine that we be in one location," says Corning Inc. President Peter F. Volanakis.

That's good news for the residents of Steuben County, where Corning is the largest employer. Since 2005 they have

Michael Mandel, Steve Hamm, and Christopher Ferrell, "Are They Good for America?" *BusinessWeek*, March 10, 2008, pp. 41–46. Copyright © 2008 by The McGraw-Hill Companies, Inc. Reprinted by special permission.

watched their unemployment rate drop faster than that of neighboring counties, in part because of Corning's commitment to the area and its ability to sell around the world.

Americans are going to need quite a few more Cornings— global companies willing to invest in the U.S.—to ease the pain of the economic slowdown. The big multinationals are the go-to guys right now: They've got plenty of cash and soaring profits from overseas operations. They're highly productive and innovative, more so than domestic companies. And unlike consumers, banks, and smaller companies, the multinationals aren't constrained by the credit crunch.

Multinationals to the Rescue?

Indeed, the top 150 U.S.-based nonfinancial multinationals, which include the likes of Hewlett-Packard, Pfizer, eBay, and Sara Lee, had more than $500 billion in cash and short-term investments at the end of 2007. Some of the big global players with extensive operations in the U.S.—companies such as Toyota and Siemens—are equally flush. By contrast, smaller domestic-oriented companies have weaker profit outlooks and more short-term debt and other liabilities on their books and therefore are having a harder time borrowing. . . .

The combination of the falling dollar and rising costs overseas is making it more appealing for high-productivity multinationals to shift some production and employment back to the U.S.

The combination of the falling dollar and rising costs overseas is making it more appealing for high-productivity multinationals to shift some production and employment back to the U.S. Such moves are already showing up in rising exports and the increased willingness of foreign companies to put their money into the U.S. Indeed, foreign direct investment in the U.S. in the third quarter of 2007 was at its highest level since 2000.

The uncertain role of the multinationals during this downturn makes Federal Reserve Chairman Ben S. Bernanke's job that much harder. His primary tool—cutting interest rates—isn't very effective with cash-rich multinationals that can already borrow on attractive terms. Moreover, the corporate executives who run the multinationals have far more on their minds than interest and exchange rates. Tax considerations, incentives from other countries, labor-force quality, and long-term corporate strategy all loom over their decisions as well. . . .

Exporting Jobs, Not Goods

Multinationals have been the wild card in the economic deck for a decade. Back in 1997, four years after the passage of the North American Free Trade Agreement, the economists at the [U.S.] Bureau of Labor Statistics [BLS] in Washington put out their biennial projections of job growth over the next 10 years. With a touching note of optimism, they assumed that exports, adjusted for inflation, would double over the next decade—a boom that would have produced a sizable number of good-paying American jobs.

But like almost everyone else, the BLS economists missed an unexpected strategy shift at the handful of big companies that account for most of the exports. Instead of ramping up American operations to sell into global markets, giant U.S. companies such as General Electric, IBM, and United Technologies took their operations overseas, expanding in Asia and Europe and becoming global enterprises with international workforces. The result: U.S. export growth fell 50% short of the BLS economists' prediction. The much prophesied job boom never happened.

In effect, U.S. multinationals have been decoupling from the U.S. economy in the past decade. They still have their headquarters in America, they're still listed on U.S. stock exchanges, and most of their shareholders are still American. But their expansion has been mainly overseas.

At Emerson Electric, for example, international sales more than doubled, to $11.6 billion, from 1997 to 2007. But exports from the U.S. rose by about 20%, to $1.3 billion. At United Technologies, which ranks among the top 20 companies in terms of foreign revenue, export revenues rose by 62%, to $6.2 billion, from 1997 to 2007. But total sales outside the U.S. jumped from $13 billion to $34 billion.

Some executives are quite clear about their strategy. "We have clients who need work done in other parts of the world to serve their clients," says Ronald A. Rittenmeyer, who serves as chairman, president, and CEO of Electronic Data Systems [EDS], which [in 2007] granted early retirement to 2,400 U.S. workers. "Our employee base will continue to shift, with the number of jobs located in high-quality, lower-cost areas outside the U.S. growing." EDS expects to have 45,000 offshore employees by the end of 2008, up from 14,000 at the end of 2005.

As the big companies have moved abroad to expand their global operations, smaller U.S. companies haven't taken their place as exporters. According to data from the [U.S.] Census Bureau, exporting is just as dominated by big companies as it ever was: In 2006 companies with 500 or more employees accounted for 71% of goods exported, the same as in 2000.

Only a relatively small number of U.S.-based corporations have established a substantial global presence. When the non-financial companies in the Standard & Poor's 1500 are ranked by their reported foreign sales, the top 150 account for 84% of the total. Virtually all of the names are easily recognizable. "There are only a few truly global companies," says John Dowdy, a partner in McKinsey's [McKinsey Global Institute, an economics research group] London office who recently helped lead a study on multinationals.

The dominance of a few top companies holds true in Europe as well. In a new report titled "The Happy Few," economists Thierry Mayer of the University of Paris and Gianmarco I.P. Ottaviano of the University of Bologna [Italy] write: "The international performance of European countries is essentially driven by a handful of high-performance firms." The same is true in Japan, where Toyota, Honda, Sony, and a few other big names carry the flag.

Multinationals are more productive, pay more, and are better managed than their domestic counterparts.

The "globalization gap"—a yawning gulf between big multinationals and everyone else—helps explain why Americans are so conflicted about trade. On the one hand, research by Dowdy and others suggests that multinationals are more productive, pay more, and are better managed than their domestic counterparts. "They are high-wage, high-productivity firms, and that's what every economy wants to have," says Andrew B. Bernard, an economist at Dartmouth's Tuck School of Business and an expert on multinationals. Bernard estimates that multinationals pay workers 6% more on average than domestic companies, while Mayer and Ottaviano find a bigger difference in most European countries.

In some industries, multinationals have cut jobs less aggressively than comparable domestic firms, perhaps because the multinationals held on to R&D [research and development] and headquarters jobs to serve the global market. From 2000 to 2005, overall employment in manufacturing fell by 18%. But U.S.-based multinationals cut by only 12.5%.

Still, multinationals are not big job producers, either in the U.S. or abroad. The top U.S.-based multinationals provided only 47% of jobs in the S&P 1500 nonfinancial companies in 2006 while accounting for 57% of the sales and 62% of the profits. These figures include all jobs, not just the domestic ones.

What's more, the government figures show that the share of domestic output generated by U.S. multinationals shrank from 21.8% of GDP [gross domestic product] in 2000 to 18.5% in 2005. It could have bounced back in the years since then, but it doesn't seem likely.

There are other paths by which the success of U.S.-based multinationals can boost the economy. One is through the stock market.

Boost to the U.S. Economy

Of course, there are other paths by which the success of U.S.-based multinationals can boost the economy. One is through the stock market. Despite large influxes of foreign money into the country, U.S. stocks are still owned mostly by Americans, either directly or through mutual funds and pension funds. The reason is simple: Foreign investors have mostly chosen to put their money into supposedly safer investments, such as U.S. Treasury securities, corporate bonds, and mortgage-backed securities, much to their dismay. As a result, foreigners own only 13% of U.S. equities, according to the Federal Reserve.

What's more, most research and product development is still done in the U.S. "The center of mass [of R&D] isn't going to suddenly move somewhere else," says Jonathan Eaton, an economist at New York University. "R&D is still extremely concentrated." In the short run, that's good news, because those kinds of jobs tend to be well-paid and relatively immune to the business cycle.

At Corning, the top executives made a conscious decision to keep virtually all of their R&D at headquarters. "We want to invest in creating a pool of expertise that is relatively stable here in Corning, N.Y.," says Mark A. Newhouse, senior vice-president for new business development. Adds David L. Morse, senior vice-president for corporate research: "This country is still the best place to do industrial research."

Even in the semiconductor industry, which has spread plants and research facilities around the world, the big U.S. companies have banded together with 25 top American universities to do research into the use of cutting-edge nanotech materials and processes. Formed in 2004, the alliance is now in full swing. "I'm confident that we'll blow through these barriers, and I'm confident the U.S. will be a leader in this industry for decades to come," says John E. Kelly III, director of research at IBM.

The alliance is spending just $70 million a year on collaborative research right now, far too little to jolt the economy out of its short-term doldrums. But over time, as the group puts its research into action, its members will spend several billion dollars implementing the changes, says Kelly. For IBM, most of its investments will be in the U.S., since its two chip plants are in East Fishkill, N.Y., and Burlington, Vt., and its largest research labs are in Westchester County, N.Y., and Silicon Valley. Says George M. Scalise, the president of the Semiconductor Industry Assn.: "Basic research and manufacturing will be more tightly woven geographically, in spite of our ability to communicate so freely via the Net."

Many economists believe a multinational's nationality is unimportant.

Nationality Question

But globalization raises other questions. Does a company's nationality matter from the perspective of the U.S. economy?

Does it matter whether jobs come from Google or Toyota? Is a U.S.-based global company any more likely to invest in the U.S. during a downturn?

Many economists believe a multinational's nationality is unimportant. "You want the jobs in the country, but it ultimately doesn't matter who owns the firms," says Nicholas Bloom, a Stanford University economist who studies multinationals. Robert B. Reich, the Labor Secretary under Bill Clinton, agrees: "Nationality matters almost not at all today."

Certainly some foreign companies have moved into the U.S. in a big way. Siemens, for example, has invested heavily in the U.S. in the past few years. That includes opening a facility making wind turbine blades in Fort Madison, Iowa, in 2007, which Siemens plans to expand. "That business is very robust in the U.S. market," says George Nolen, president and CEO of Siemens Corp., the U.S. subsidiary of the German multinational.

There are lots of spillover effects from having the headquarters of a global company in a town, including monetary support for local colleges, museums, hospitals, and other nonprofit activities.

Others believe those stateside expansions serve the U.S. better when the multinationals are U.S.-owned. "The reality is that the value chain tends to keep the knowledge and expertise near the center," says Christopher A. Bartlett, a professor at Harvard Business School. "I'd prefer to have U.S. multinational companies."

The success of U.S.-based multinationals can also affect the quality of life in parts of the country where they have a big presence. In particular, there are lots of spillover effects from having the headquarters of a global company in a town, including monetary support for local colleges, museums, hospitals, and other nonprofit activities.

Hutchinson, Minn., home to Hutchinson Technology, illustrates the link between global success of a U.S.-based company and its impact on a local community. The maker of high-precision disk-drive components, which now sells about 90% of its output outside the U.S., was co-founded in 1965 by a Hutchinson native. "The local ownership has had a tremendous impact on the local community," says Mike Boehme, chairman of the board of the Hutchinson Chamber of Commerce and a dean at Ridgewater College in town. "If a foreign group took over, we wouldn't be the community we are."

Cost-Benefit Analyses

The lack of jobs and investment coming from U.S. multinationals didn't matter too much during the housing boom. Even as U.S. jobs at global firms slumped, domestic employers in construction, health care, and restaurants took up the slack.

But now Americans—and the Fed—need the multinationals to help out. Will they start investing enough in this country to cushion the downturn? The value of the dollar [as of early 2008] has fallen by more than 20% against the currencies of U.S. trading partners since 2003, the biggest sustained decline since the index was started in 1973. In particular, the dollar has dropped by 15% against the Chinese yuan. Meanwhile, labor costs in China and India have jumped, while real wages in the U.S. have fallen by 1% in the past year [2007–2008], according to an experimental index that covers all jobs, even the highest-paid ones. Transportation costs have risen as well, making shipping more costly. All of that makes producing in the U.S. more attractive today than it has been in a while.

But the chief executives of multinationals don't make location decisions based on short-term economic fundamentals alone. For one thing, they worry about taxes. The U.S. has one of the highest corporate income tax rates among industrialized nations, according to data from the Organization for Economic Cooperation & Development.

Moving operations overseas gives a multinational an almost infinite number of legal and quasi-legal strategies for reducing U.S. corporate taxes. It can borrow in high-tax countries to take maximum advantage of interest-rate deductions; it can transfer intellectual property to low-tax countries, in exchange for below-market royalty payments; and when it ships goods to its foreign affiliates, it can charge low prices to shift profits to low-tax jurisdictions. The result is that collections of U.S. corporate income taxes have been dropping significantly as a share of total global profits for U.S. companies. "Companies have taken advantage of these favorable cost-shifting agreements," says Jack Mutti, an economist at Iowa's Grinnell College and an international tax expert. "The law gets so complicated that very few people can understand what the trade-offs are."

Big Tax Shift?

To encourage multinational expansion in the U.S., it may be necessary to revise the corporate tax system, a step for which there is surprising support from Democrats and Republicans alike. One proposal—with the arcane name "formulary apportionment"—would tax the earnings of multinationals based on the proportion of their customer base in the U.S. For example, under this system it's possible a U.S. company that only exported would pay virtually no corporate income taxes, while a foreign company that was a big importer to the U.S. would pay a hefty chunk of change on its worldwide income. Other economists believe the corporate income tax hasn't adjusted to the global economy and think it should be eliminated.

The other big question is whether the U.S. needs to subsidize multinationals to entice them to keep jobs in the U.S. That comes up a lot in industries such as semiconductors, which require heavy capital investment. "We have to choose to compete on the investment level and match other countries' offerings on incentives and tax breaks," says Scalise of the Semiconductor Industry Assn. "If we don't do this, it will be very difficult for us to maintain our leadership in technology and innovation." Adds Hector Ruiz, CEO of Advanced Micro Devices: "It's not corporate welfare. [This is] a competitive world."

Perhaps the smartest long-term policy would be to cultivate future multinationals. The real boost to national economies comes from the formation of new multinationals, which in their early hypergrowth years create an enormous number of jobs and put down deep roots. No American would deny that the U.S. is better off because Google started there rather than somewhere else. The European economists Mayer and Ottaviano argue that policymakers shouldn't "waste time helping the incumbent superstars." Instead, they should "nurture the superstars of the future." That may mean simplifying the amazingly complicated system for taxing multinationals, which both collects relatively low revenue and imposes big compliance costs. "Put in place as few barriers as possible for all companies," says Bernard. "The good ones will rise to the top."

These new multinationals of the future won't arrive in time to help the U.S. in this credit crunch, however. It's going to be the big multinationals of the present who will—or won't—make the difference.

11

Outsourcing Creates a Need to Revamp the U.S. Education System

Maggie Nassif and William Roe

Maggie Nassif has a PhD from Cairo University and serves as the director of the Arabic summer masters of business administration program for the Wharton School of Business/Lauder Institute in Pennsylvania. William Roe has a PhD from Mississippi State University and serves as the director of graduate business programs at Arkansas State University.

An Arkansas State University study revealed the U.S. education system is not competitive when compared with the education systems of Europe and Asia. According to the study, the United States needs to revamp its education system to be a superpower in the global marketplace. A greater emphasis on science, math, geography, and foreign languages is needed to reduce the outsourcing of high-paying jobs. Governments and corporations should work with colleges, universities, and vocational schools to prepare the workforce.

The financial ramifications of off-shoring service jobs to Asia may be uncertain, but its impact on vocational training in the USA is eminent. The USA needs a comprehensive strategy for preparing its future global workforce. The main questions on economists' minds remain: what is the world going to look like in the next two decades? Where will the USA

Maggie Nassif and William Roe, "Who Moved My Job?" *Competitiveness Review*, vol. 19, Winter/Spring 2009, p. 36(10). Copyright © 2009 Emerald Group Publishing, Ltd. Reproduced by permission.

be compared to other emerging World Powers in 2020? Does the USA have a strategy to influence the future to the benefit of its own human capital? To answer these questions one needs to look at key issues shaping the evolution of the global workforce in the twenty-first century: outsourcing as an opportunity; the race among China, India, and other new emerging competitors; the increasing loss of jobs and drop in college enrollment in certain majors in the USA; and the effect of these trends on geopolitical dynamics. In the midst of all these looming threats emerges an inspiring model from a rural campus that seems to have formulated a possible academic solution: rural outsourcing. . . .

India and China currently produce 500,000 engineers a year while in the USA the number is 60,000.

Higher Education

As Americans start to compete for jobs globally, the U.S. education system regretfully may seem complacent, when compared to education in Europe and Asia, which emphasizes science, math, geography, and foreign languages. A 1998 OECD [Organisation for Economic Co-Operation and Development] study indicated that American schools ranked second to last among industrialized nations in teaching science. At the higher education level, India and China currently produce 500,000 engineers a year while in the USA the number is 60,000. India alone graduates 70,000 accountants per year. In addition, national figures show a disturbing drop in IT [information technology] and engineering enrollments. The danger is that as IT jobs continue to be outsourced to India, this may cause more of a drop in enrollment in these fields due to the fear of unemployment as a result of outsourcing. However, although these developments may be unsettling, change always presents new opportunities.

At Arkansas State University [ASU] where the total enrollment of CIT [computer and information technology] majors dropped from 322 students in 2001 down to 173 in 2004, Professor John Seydel, Chair of the Department of Computer and Information Technology, observes that the hiring of IT specialists is indeed going back up after the e-commerce boom and bust of the 1990s, especially in such areas as IT security and project management. In a personal interview in February 2006 at the ASU campus Seydel noted:

> Students need to have more sophisticated skills now to be competitive, not just be able to write a program. At this point it seems too late in the game to discuss whether we can stop outsourcing; rather we need to design programs to train American students to compete for available openings to manage outsourcing [. . .]. The new competency in IT organization is managing a portfolio of suppliers in an integrated fashion.

According to a 2005 Deloitte Consulting LLP study, "the general outsourcing failure rate is more than 70%." Perhaps that is why this rural campus in Arkansas seems to be taking positive steps towards developing such training programs to better equip its local workforce for global competition and provide opportunities for . . . "back sourcing." This may be made possible by India's trouble in addressing issues associated with sustaining growth, such as overcoming the rising shortage of engineers, inflated wages, and the high-attrition rates that are affecting the Indian workforce. Indian BPOs [business process outsourcing] have already started operations in China and Hungary to tap into the local talent.

This is an opportunity to "back source" some IT jobs and create a niche for a new demographics of IT workers who are strategically positioned halfway between the Silicon Valley workers and those in Bangalore. The question is how? And there is no easy answer. An American computer engineer who earns $70,000 a year will have to drastically differentiate his/ her skills from an Indian engineer who earns $8,000.

Rural Sourcing

Rural Sourcing is an IT company that was launched in 2003 in Jonesboro, Arkansas, in partnership with Arkansas State University. Rural Sourcing addresses two crucial issues, that of higher education as well as employment. It all started when Kathy White, an Arkansas State University alumna who had to relocate from her native Arkansas to North Carolina for an academic job, came back to Arkansas with an idea that would generate job opportunities for the local Jonesboro population. White, who is a former member of both academia and corporate America, wanted to use her expertise for the mutual benefit of both work fields. Kathy White started as a Professor at the University of North Carolina at Greensboro, then left academia eventually to become Executive Vice-President and Chief Information Officer at Cardinal Health, Inc., a $65 billion healthcare company, in the Midwest. It was then that she set up a virtual internship for business students at Arkansas State University at Cardinal Health.

At 52, armed with $2,000,000 of her own money, White partnered with Arkansas State University at Jonesboro to set up Rural Sourcing, Inc. The idea is simple: instead of outsourcing jobs to India, send them to Jonesboro, Arkansas, where the median household income is $32,196. She knew she would operate at an average of 30 percent lower rates than her Silicon Valley competitors.

She also would have no problem staffing her project from the approximately 30 IT graduates that ASU's main campus in Jonesboro pumps out every year. To facilitate the partnership, she founded the Horizon Institute of Technology Foundation in 2003 to support economic and workforce development in the Delta [the environs of Jonesboro]. The project headquarters was housed in the ASU small business incubator where the Jonesboro branch still operates under the supervision of Henry Torres, Director of Business Development and Senior IT Lecturer at ASU. Torres is in charge of recruiting and job preparedness training of ASU talent for the company. "Although we have not been able to raise enrollment, our accomplishments are obvious in the field of curriculum development," Torres states;

> Our students needed more depth of knowledge, so we met with the IT curriculum committee and we added extra advanced courses as a requirement in certain IT topics the students study. The aim is to train students on the job to fill the immediate and emerging needs of the market. Rural Sourcing is doing so by using its competitive advantages having professors/consultants use their firsthand knowledge of the American market, and industry standards, to train "a new breed of offshore BPO provider." These are "partners not vendors, providers who build brands that differentiate themselves" and not just offer "labor arbitrage and commodity-like service."

When I toured Rural Sourcing facilities in 2006, Torres, a former WalMart and Frederick's of Hollywood top executive was very optimistic. He stated, "There is so much potential out there. Our core competence is that we think like a big company, but we do it at a small town cost." With so much potential, Rural Sourcing conducted an internal strategic study to identify their niche market and brand their services. They have decided for the time being to concentrate on internal applications. Over 90 percent of their projects have been intranet/Web-based application development and support, such as Executive Dashboard, Legacy System Integration, and Information Portal.

Although Rural Sourcing has just started breaking even in its second year, the company is experiencing healthy growth and some international recognition. With 25 employees in seven centers, spread over five states, all partnered with higher education institutes, it is not unlikely that the company will achieve its ten year goal of 50 centers in 20 states. The question remains, can the Rural Sourcing model be duplicated in other rural areas in the South and the Midwest where cost is relatively low and unemployment is high? Can it be the answer to off-shoring? Can Jonesboro compete with Bangalore? The main hurdle remains higher cost.

American industries will find it in their long-term interest to train sophisticated knowledge workers and retain some operations stateside.

It costs $58 an hour to get a job done in San Francisco, $40 in Jonesboro and $12 in India. However, there are two hopeful points to make here. American industries will find it in their long-term interest to train sophisticated knowledge workers and retain some operations stateside to protect the privacy of their customers and dominance over its know-how. Also as these rural initiatives evolve, they will achieve economies of scale and its workforce will better differentiate their services from those done in Bangalore, which brings the issue back to education and training. The problems with outsourcing are many, but they may be grouped into three main categories: strategy, security and employment. The solution to all three problems lies in future planning and investment in education and vocational training for new generations of knowledge workers who can resolve these problems.

IT as Strategic Weapon

Before companies outsource IT to concentrate on core competency, they need to assess the importance of IT as a strategic weapon. As [Gifford] Pinchot and [Elizabeth] Pinchot pose the question in their book *The End of Bureaucracy and the Rise of the Intelligent Organization*, "This creates a genuine dilemma: how to create strategies for core competence that cross several business units without returning to a system of centralized planning and control." Losing know-how on certain operations can prove damaging to the individual firm or industry, as well as to the national economy. The solution is to train American knowledge workers at a high-enough level to be able to manage and oversee these outsourced functions. This training involves technical as well as linguistic and cultural understanding of the world's civilizations and international markets.

The higher [an employee's] training, the longer America can hold on to its position as the strongest economy in the world.

Security Risks

Outsourcing results in disposing of the responsibility of functions but also surrendering control to another company, whether it is US-based or abroad. Off-shoring is therefore especially alarming when it comes to securing sensitive information such as financial data and medical records. Although India passed the IT Act in 2000 to protect intellectual property and customer privacy, the standards still do not meet E.C. [European Community] and US approval, and enforcement of these rules leaves a lot to be desired. The most alarming threat was of alleged plans of the Pakistani militant group Lashkar-e-Taiba to attack US interests in Bangalore in March [2009]. The incident was followed by two hoaxes at the headquarters of Wipro and Infosys. Regardless of the real level of threat, just the thought of such an incident still raises the question: how do we secure main arteries that support the economy of the homeland if they are outsourced out of the homeland? Homeland security has been offering generous scholarships as an educational solution to face this problem. These scholarships have produced highly trained IT engineers who study and develop virtual security barriers which are used to protect personal as well as corporate financial assets.

Redefining Employment

This is the biggest problem and where the most promising potential lies. As economic prosperity and full employment go hand in hand, the biggest threat of outsourcing remains job loss among highly trained and well-paid service employees. With the loss of jobs go disposable income, confident spending, and the resulting . . . effect that it has on the local economy. Besides the financial loss there are also technical and strategic losses. As [John] Worthington defined the office in functional terms in his book, *Reinventing the Workplace*, he wrote, "In the future, IT will become the driver of organizational success." Simultaneously, the functions and relations of employees with the firm are also being redefined and so is their training. The higher their training, the longer America can hold on to its position as the strongest economy in the world, in this age of major reconfiguration of powers anticipated within the next two decades. In this highly competitive race, the global worker of the twenty-first century is a proactive employee who is willing to retrain, relocate and even go out on his/her own. The whole social contract between the employer and employee is being redefined. According to [Andrew and Nada] Kakabadse [in their book *Smart Sourcing*], the new employee possesses the following traits:

- career resilience;

- self-responsibility for designing career;

- self-reliance;

- trust in self and network;

- personal flexibility; and

- expansion of skills to stay competitive.

Hence, the new role of the corporation has become to provide tools and opportunities for assessing and developing skills. Similarly, the job of parents, community leaders, government officials and business leaders is to collaborate on revamping a US education system that equips students to compete in a virtual workplace that is not restricted by visas and work permits. This workplace requires its worker to be:

- bilingual;

- able to navigate a multi-cultural environment; and

- good at math and science.

There are currently 28 states that have drafted initiatives . . . to integrate or require foreign language in their K–12 education system.

As American educators and policy makers realize both the gravity of the situation and the immensity of potential of this demand, there are various opportunities (old and new) that are being made available for students to identify and support talent in the fields of math, science and foreign languages. In January of 2006, President [George W.] Bush approved a comprehensive national plan: The National Security Language Initiative, to expand US foreign language education beginning in early childhood (kindergarten) and continuing throughout formal schooling and into the workforce with new programs and resources. The program focuses its $230 million budget towards educating students, teachers and government workers in critical-need foreign languages, such as Arabic, Chinese, Hindi and Farsi, and increasing the number of advanced-level speakers in those and other languages. More attention is being paid to the importance of international education: there are currently 28 states that have drafted initiatives to assess and improve teaching and learning about the different regions of the world and to integrate or require foreign language in their

K–12 education system. In addition, The National Security Agency has for years been holding summer math and science camps for middle- and high-school students as well as offering internship opportunities for university students to support and identify young talent. One is hopeful that all these resources and efforts are being utilized to bring the American education system up to par with the rest of the industrialized world and that global vocational training would start in the K–12 system as opposed to higher education.

The obvious remedy to the potential dangers of outsourcing . . . can be attained through both government and corporate supported initiatives to strategically partner corporate America with academia.

In closing, outsourcing between the East and the West is not a new phenomenon; the British outsourced production of cotton, spices and tea to India in the seventeenth century. In the nineteenth century, they expanded their cotton operations to Egypt and their tea to China, but now the story is reversed and power seems to be shifting. It is up to the USA to choose its place in the twenty-first century. Since, as Mike Hoyt, CEO of Paradigm Works, stated, "To outsource/offshore is not a political decision on the part of the company, it is an economic decision with political ramifications." The obvious remedy to the potential dangers of outsourcing beyond American borders can be attained through both government and corporate supported initiatives to strategically partner corporate America with academia as in the case of Rural Sourcing.

Organizations to Contact

The editors have compiled the following list of organizations concerned with the issues debated in this book. The descriptions are derived from materials provided by the organizations. All have publications or information available for interested readers. The list was compiled on the date of publication of the present volume; the information provided here may change. Be aware that many organizations take several weeks or longer to respond to inquiries, so allow as much time as possible.

American Federation of Labor and Congress of Industrial Organizations (AFL-CIO)
815 Sixteenth St. NW, Washington, DC 20006
Web site: www.aflcio.org

The American Federation of Labor and Congress of Industrial Organizations is a voluntary federation of fifty-five national and international labor unions. The mission of the AFL-CIO is to improve the lives of working families—to bring economic justice to the workplace and social justice to the nation. Its Web site is designed to inspire and support frontline union leaders and activists with tips, tools, and news to build a strong voice for U.S. working families.

Brookings Institution
1775 Massachusetts Ave. NW, Washington, DC 20036
(202) 797-6000
Web site: www.brookings.edu

The mission of the Brookings Institution is to conduct high-quality independent research and, based on that research, to provide innovative, practical recommendations that advance three broad goals: strengthening U.S. democracy; fostering the economic and social welfare, security, and opportunity of all Americans; and securing a more open, safe, prosperous, and cooperative international system. Its publications include *Offshoring, Import Competition, and the Jobless Recovery*; *The Outsourcing Bogeyman*; *Hardheaded Optimism About Globalization*; and *Offshoring Service Jobs: Bane or Boon—and What to Do?*

Center for Global Outsourcing (CGO)
26 Berkley Blvd., Iselin, NJ   08830
(732) 983-7034
Web site: www.outsourceglobal.org

The mission of the Center for Global Outsourcing is to advance knowledge of the benefits of global outsourcing to businesses and to help businesses understand how to realize the improvements in productivity that global outsourcing offers. The center holds annual conferences to facilitate direct communication between client company managers, vendor company managers, government/embassy officials, industry leaders, and academicians, thus reducing the information gap that exists between them. The center sponsors three industry journals: the *Journal of Information Technology: Case and Application Research*; *Journal of Global Information Technology Management*; and the *Journal of Information Privacy and Security*.

National Association of Manufacturers (NAM)
1331 Pennsylvania Ave. NW, Washington, DC   20004-1790
(202) 637-3000 • fax: (202) 637-3182
Web site: www.nam.org

NAM's mission is to advocate on behalf of its members to enhance the competitiveness of manufacturers by shaping a legislative and regulatory environment conducive to U.S. economic growth and to increase understanding among policy makers, the media, and the general public about the vital role manufacturing plays in U.S. economic and national security. NAM is a primary source for information on manufacturers' contributions to innovation and productivity. *Capital Briefing* is the flagship weekly e-news briefing of NAM.

National Bureau of Economic Research, Inc. (NBER)
1050 Massachusetts Ave., Cambridge, MA   02138
(617) 868-3900 • fax: (617) 868-2742
Web site: www.nber.org

Founded in 1920, the National Bureau of Economic Research is a private nonprofit, nonpartisan research organization dedicated to promoting a greater understanding of how the economy works. NBER is committed to undertaking and disseminating unbiased economic research among public-policy makers, business professionals, and the academic community. NBER publications include the *NBER Digest, NEBR Reporter,* and *International Trade in Services and Intangibles in the Era of Globalization.*

U.S. Bureau of Labor Statistics (BLS)
2 Massachusetts Ave. NE, Washington, DC   20212-0001
(202) 691-5200
Web site: www.bls.gov

As part of the U.S. Department of Labor, the Bureau of Labor Statistics is the principal fact-finding agency for the federal government in the broad field of labor economics and statistics. BLS publications include *Occupational Employment Projections to 2012* and *The 1988–2000 Employment Projections: How Accurate Were They?*

U.S. Consumer Product Safety Commission (CPSC)
4330 East-West Hwy., Bethesda, MD   20814
(301) 504-7923 • fax: (301) 504-0124
Web site: www.cpsc.gov

The U.S. Consumer Product Safety Commission is charged with protecting the public from unreasonable risks of serious injury or death from thousands of types of consumer products under the agency's jurisdiction. Its work to ensure the safety of consumer products—such as toys, cribs, power tools, cigarette lighters, and household chemicals—contributed significantly to the 30 percent decline in the rate of deaths and injuries associated with consumer products over the past thirty years. The CPSC's monthly e-newsletter *Safety Review* offers an in-depth look at the latest hazards associated with home and recreational products, as well as the most significant current product recalls.

World Trade Organization (WTO)

Centre William Rappard, Rue de Lausanne 154
Geneva 21, Switzerland   CH-1211
41 22 739 51 11 • fax: 41 22 731 42 06
Web site: www.wto.org

The World Trade Organization is an international organization dealing with the rules of trade between nations. It has as its foundation the WTO agreements, negotiated and signed by the majority of the world's trading nations. WTO publications include *World Trade Report*, an annual publication that aims to deepen understanding about trends in trade, trade policy issues, and the multilateral trading system.

Bibliography

Books

Paul Bergin, Robert C. Feenstra, Gordon H. Hanson — *Outsourcing and Volatility.* Cambridge, MA: National Bureau of Economic Research, 2007.

Douglas Brown and Scott Wilson — *The Black Book of Outsourcing: How to Manage the Changes, Challenges, and Opportunities.* Hoboken, NJ: John Wiley, 2005.

Jack Buffington — *An Easy Out: Corporate America's Addiction to Outsourcing.* Westport, CT: Praeger, 2007.

Jacqueline Ching — *Outsourcing U.S. Jobs.* New York: Rosen, 2009.

Stephen Currie — *Outsourcing in America.* Yankton, SD: Erickson, 2007.

Paul Davies — *What's This India Business? Offshoring, Outsourcing, and the Global Services Revolution.* Yarmouth, ME: Nicholas Brealey International, 2008.

Jody Freeman — *Government by Contract: Outsourcing and American Democracy.* Cambridge, MA: Harvard University Press, 2009.

Ron French — *Driven Abroad: The Outsourcing of America.* Muskegon, MI: RDR Books, 2006.

Ron Hira and Anil Hira — *Outsourcing America: The True Cost of Shipping Jobs Overseas and What Can Be Done About It.* New York: AMACOM, 2008.

Harbhajan S. Kehal and Varinder P. Singh, eds. — *Outsourcing and Offshoring in the 21st Century: A Socio-Economic Perspective.* Hershey, PA: Idea Group, 2006.

Mark Kobayashi-Hillary, ed. — *Building a Future with BRICs: The Next Decade for Offshoring.* New York: Springer, 2008.

Thomas M. Koulopoulos and Tom Roloff — *Smartsourcing: Driving Innovation and Growth Through Outsourcing.* Avon, MA: Platinum Press/Adams Media, 2006.

Eva Paus — *Global Capitalism Unbound: Winners and Losers from Offshore Outsourcing.* New York: Palgrave Macmillan, 2009.

Ruth Taplin, ed. — *Outsourcing and Human Resource Management: An International Survey.* New York: Routledge, 2007.

Atul Vashistha and Avinash Vashistha — *The Offshore Nation: Strategies for Success in Global Outsourcing and Offshoring.* New York: McGraw-Hill, 2006.

Periodicals

Charles L. Aird and Derek Sappenfield — "IT the 'Enabler' of Global Outsourcing," *Financial Executive*, June 1, 2009.

Alan Beattie	"Free-Traders Conspicuously Quiet on Buy American," *Financial Times*, February 6, 2009.
Geoffrey Colvin	"America Isn't Ready [Here's What to Do About It]," *Fortune*, July 25, 2005.
Richard Ernsberger Jr.	"The Big Squeeze; A 'Second Wave' of Offshoring Could Threaten Middle-Income, White-Collar, and Skilled Blue-Collar Jobs," *Newsweek International*, May 30, 2005.
James Fallows	"China Makes, the World Takes," *Atlantic*, July/August 2007.
Phil Fersht, Dana Stiffler, and Kevin O'Marah	"The Ins and Outs of Offshoring," *Supply Chain Management Review*, March 1, 2009.
Steven Greenhouse	"Offshoring Silicon Valley," *American Prospect*, May 27, 2008.
Ken Hoffman	"All the Way to India for Computer Help," *Houston Chronicle*, March 14, 2008.
William F. Jasper	"Good-bye to Independence?" *New American*, February 7, 2005.
George Leopold	"Offshoring Backlash Rises as Layoffs Mount," *Electronic Engineering Times*, March 23, 2009.
Michael Mandel and Pete Engardio	"The Real Cost of Offshoring," *BusinessWeek*, June 18, 2007.

Stephanie Overby   "The Truth About Obama's 'Tax on Outsourcing,'" *CIO*, May 12, 2009.

Art Pulaski   "Point of View: Outsourcing Jobs During Recession," *Ontario (CA) Inland Valley Bulletin*, May 1, 2008.

Tyson B. Roan   "Anything but Doomed: Why Restrictions on Offshoring Are Permissible Under the Constitution and Trade Agreements," *Employee Rights and Employment Policy Journal*, 2009.

Neil Shister   "Integrating the Global Supply Chain," *World Trade*, May 28, 2006.

Rajeev Srinivasan   "The Impact of U.S. Protectionism," and Remitha   *India Currents*, March 13, 2009.
Satheesh

Patrick   "Experts: Tax Changes Won't Curb Thibodeau   Offshoring," *Computerworld*, May 11, 2009.

Perry A. Trunick   "The Rise of Outsourcing," *Logistics Today*, June 1, 2008.

Douglas Turner   "Will Congress, Obama Stop Outsourcing Jobs?" *Buffalo (NY) News*, December 16, 2008.

Index

[2]